JesusPerfect

To Dr. Oster,

   With much thankfulness
for your help w/ this book,
and for holding up such
a high standard for
Biblical scholarship.

        In Him,.

        Jim Stes

        Phil. 2:3-4 !

JesusPerfect

Jimmy Sites

Christian Communications
P. O. Box 150
Nashville, TN 37202

Unless otherwise indicated, all Scripture quotations are from the Holy Bible, New International Version, copyright © 1973, 1978 by the International Bible Society. Used by permission.

Sharing the thoughts of his own heart, the author may express views not entirely consistent with those of the publisher.

Book design by Gregory A. Needels

Artwork by Rick Gibson

Cover design by Joel A. Butts

©1994 by Christian Communications

Published by Christian Communications
P. O. Box 150
Nashville, TN 37202
1-800-251-8446

Printed in the United States of America

Contents

To my daughter, Christin;
if I had a penny for every
ounce of love I have for you,
I would be a millionaire.

Inadvertantly left out by printer. Will be in 2nd printing.

ACKNOWLEDGMENTS

A special thanks to:

Neil and Kerry Anderson and the Gospel Advocate staff for believing in the effectiveness of the printed page.

Mark McInteer -- for believing in my dreams from the very beginning.

Larry Weeden -- A good editor is a poor writer's best asset. Thanks for the help.

Terry Groves, Dr. Richard Oster, Christina Pyktel, Mom and Dad, and the guys in ACAPPELLA -- for working your way through this material and fine-tuning it.

Dr. Lynn Anderson -- Your "support package" meant more than words can express. Good timing!

Dr. Doug Brown -- Thank you for teaching me and befriending me. Our time together in study and in reworking this book are memories I will always cherish and benefit from.

Rick Gibson -- Your drawings are the diamond in the middle of the rough. Thanks for adding roses to the stem.

St. Louis youth ministers Steve Awtrey, Mike Runcie, and Joe Taylor -- for initially planting the concept for this book in my heart (and for the fun time watching the Cardinals when I was in St. Louis!).

The teens and youth leaders in Canton (Ohio), Seattle, and Little Rock -- for taking time to fill out the questionnaire at the youth seminars and offering invaluable feedback concerning this material. Also to Jody Rhoten and Dr. Everett Huffard for compiling and analyzing the data.

Lou Seckler and the Mexico mission teams of the past summers -- *Te amo mucho!*

Phillip Menz and the wonderful Hilsborough church on the island of Carriacou, West Indies -- You showed me what true commitment really is.

The Marianna church of Christ in Marianna, Arkansas; the Southwest church of Christ in Jonesboro, Arkansas; and the Pleasant Ridge church of Christ in Arlington, Texas -- for having the faith to hire me and for allowing me the freedom to learn from my mistakes. I love you all.

The Ridge Gang -- Dr. John Cannon, Jr., Larry Carrell, Pat Malone, Mike Monroe, and Dr. Mike Walker. You guys made going to work almost as much fun as going home. I miss those Spring Creek staff lunches!

Carol Malone, Edith Mitchell, and Susan Reed -- You're the world's greatest secretaries. Also to Sarah Taylor for the total reorganization of my filing system. (I'm as sorry as you are that it all burned up two months later!)

The Hillsboro elders in Nashville, Tennessee, and Chuck Hickman and the Campaign America television crew -- It's great to work with dreamers who let go and let God!

Devlin Donaldson and the wonderful folks at Compassion International -- Thanks for the special days in Colorado Springs. Devlin, let's invade Detroit again sometime! Also, thanks to all of those who are sponsoring children in Third World countries.

My T.N.T.! (Tuesday Night Together) prayer warriors. You young men and young ladies are warriors for the Lord. Keep marching on your knees!

Max Lucado -- You are a master with words because of your Master with the Word. His Son really shines through your pen. Thanks for the help on my previous book.

A special thanks to some very special people who prefer to remain anonymous. Your generosity and commitment are making this writing ministry possible. God bless you!

My wonderful friends: Shawn, Beth Ann, Jon, "Bzurt," Willie, Trish, Jeff, Susan and Tracy, Steve and Kelly, Dava and family, Chris and Terry, Sandi, Jerry, Tom and Tricia, Doc Gaylon and Melissa, Charles, Del and Mal, the five "youth guys" at P.R., Lisa and Michelle, and my wonderful sister Debbie. *"A faithful friend is beyond price; his worth is more than money can buy"* (Ecclesiasticus 6:15).

Christin and Jonathan -- You are God's gifts of joy. I love you.

Mandy -- If I could do it all over again and again, I'd marry you a thousand times.

Jehovah God -- You are my Best Friend. Thanks for the heart transplant.

And thank you for taking time to read this book. I pray that it will point you closer to the One who really matters.

Introduction

One morning I was rummaging around in the attic of my house. Mandy had asked me to retrieve the box of old dress-up clothes she used to play with as a child. She had decided that it was time to hand them down to our daughter, Christin.

I was having a great time in the musty crawl space over the garage. My flashlight brought a smile to my face when it lit up a bag of duck decoys over in the corner. I remembered the many brisk mornings spent in the flooded timbers of eastern Arkansas with my dad teaching me how to blow a duck call.

My light moved from the decoys to a "For Sale" sign. It was the sign from the front yard of the first house we ever bought. My heart warmed up as I remembered the take-out Chinese dinner that Mandy and I ate in the empty house to celebrate the approval of the contract.

The flashlight searched on, looking for the box upon which would be written the words "Play Clothes."

I crawled over an old bed frame and brushed away a spider web that lit up like a prism in the beam of light.

Then I noticed the box. It wasn't the one labeled "Play Clothes." Rather, it was an unlabeled box. I didn't recognize it. I racked my brain trying to remember what was packed in it, but I couldn't recollect anything. My curiosity finally got the best of me.

Carefully working my way across the rafters, I reached the box and discovered that it was sealed tightly with silver duct tape. I peeled back one of the tape corners and pulled off a long strip. The box lid opened to reveal hundreds of foam peanuts. Whatever was in this box, it was certainly protected well.

I didn't really want to make a mess in my attic by digging through the foam peanuts, but I just couldn't resist finding out what was in the middle of the box. So my hands disappeared into a sea of little white squeaky things and I felt around for a clue. My right hand soon discovered one. It felt like a television. I grasped it and pulled upward, peanuts going everywhere.

At first glimpse, I remembered.

It had been years earlier when I had packed the old Tandy TRS-80 computer. It was the first of its kind. A high-priced, low-memory personal computer that Mandy's father had bought for her when she was still in high school. A computer that is now obsolete in every sense of the word.

I remember packing it so well because I wanted to preserve it as a functioning antique for the grandchildren I hoped to someday have. I put it back in the box, replaced the peanuts, and once again sealed it with duct tape.

After finishing my honey-do in the attic, I walked into my library and sat down at my work station where I began typing the words you are now reading on a Compaq lap-top computer.

Several thoughts came to mind as I typed. Computers have come a long way. This lap-top has thousands of times more memory than that first old Tandy model. Numerous computer programs are now available and affordable that are almost limitless in capability. Just about every household in America has a computer of some kind. Even kindergartens have work stations for five-year-olds to learn the basic functions of a computer. The reality is that we live in a computer-saturated society.

The Analogy

Because most of us are computer literate or at least computer conscious, I have chosen to use the analogy of a computer to teach the message of this book. Thus the title and subtitle. The pages of this book are full of important thoughts drawn from the exciting gospel of Mark — the gospel of action! Section 3 of this book is derived from a passage in the gospel of Luke that doesn't have a parallel in Mark. It supplies information that Mark doesn't offer. These two biographies of Jesus offer some remarkable and life-changing teachings.

By using the analogy of a computer, I shall attempt to compare the teachings of Mark and Luke to three basic steps in operating a computer — plugging it in to the power outlet, loading a program, and printing out the input, resulting in a completed product for others to see. Similarly, the three sections of this book are:

Section 1: Plug in to the Power
Section 2: Load God's Program
Section 3: Print Out in to Action

Much of this material has been presented to more than 35,000 teens in recent years in Nashville, Tenn.; St. Louis; Oklahoma City; Seattle; Canton (Ohio and Texas); Guadalajara; Dallas; and other cities. A questionnaire was completed by several of those teenagers and their youth leaders to aid in evaluating and fine-tuning the material. It has been tried and tested on the front lines and in the trenches. Suggestions from several biblical scholars and wordsmiths have also proved invaluable. Your feedback would also be helpful for future editions. Send your ideas to Christian Communications, P.O. Box 150, Nashville, TN 37202. They'll make sure I get your notes.

At the end of each chapter are some questions called "Process and Output." These are designed to help you apply the contents of the chapter to your life. I suggest you write your answers and thoughts in these sections. You might also keep a journal as a supplement to this book. Whatever approach you choose, be sure it includes the Word. Don't let this book or any other take the place of your daily Bible reading. Be still and listen to God every day as He communicates to you through His Word. As the psalmist wrote concerning God, "The law from your mouth is more precious to me than thousands of pieces of silver and gold."[1]

Enough of formal introductions. It's time now for you to sit down at the computer terminal of your life, pick up the electrical cord of your being, and plug in to the power source.

Jimmy Sites

ENDNOTES

1. Psalm 119:72; also Psalm 19:9-10.

Section 1
Mark 15:33-16:6a

Plug in to the Power

1 Plug in to the Power!

A sliver of light shot through the crack in the window blinds and found its way to my left eyelid. Awakened, I opened my eyes and sat halfway up on the top bunk bed, resting on my elbow. I blinked the blur out of my eyes and looked around the room, trying to remember what day it was. Then it hit me.

I must have gone to sleep while listening for the pitter-patter of Santa's reindeer on the roof. It was Christmas morning! I threw back the covers, jumped to the wooden floor below, and scampered into the living room.

I knew immediately that he had been there. Large bites had been taken from the cookies and half the milk was gone from the glass. And there was the note: *"Thanks, from Santa!"* I wheeled around and saw that my stocking was no longer empty but full of candy canes and goodies.

Then my anticipating gaze moved toward the tree. Would it be there? Had Santa remembered? Bingo! There it was. My eyes lit up like prisms in sunlight and my little four-year-old hands began tearing into the box. I was the proud recipient of a long-awaited Tyco electric race car track!

That was a Christmas I'll never forget. Was it because the electric race track was so special? Not exactly. I guess I need to finish the story.

Mom and Dad heard my squeals of delight and came to the living room, where they helped me assemble the track. We completed our task, hooked up the power control button, and placed the race car on the track. The car had a metal pin on the bottom of it that fit into the groove of the track. In the groove were metal bands through which electricity flowed causing the car to run when the power control button was pushed.

My dad plugged the power cord into the wall socket. Everything was set. Excitement was in the air. I was just about to push the power control button when the inevitable happened — our neighbors dropped by to see what Santa had delivered. The doorbell rang and my mom and dad headed for the door to greet our neighbors, leaving me sitting in the middle of my new electric race car track.

> *Like the electric race car track, you can experience a constant flow of energizing electricity when you plug in to the power of Jesus Christ.*

To this day, I still don't know why my dad said what he said. Just before he went through the door into the other room, he stopped and said, "Son, whatever you do, don't *lick* the electric race car track."

Maybe Bill Cosby is right about his theory of intergenerational depravity — kids will sometimes do just the opposite of what their parents ask. And that's exactly what I did. No sooner had my father's heel disappeared around that door frame than my tongue ejected from my mouth and thrust itself straight into the groove of that electric race car track.

To say that was a shocking experience is putting it mildly! *Energizing* might be a better word. There was a muffled pop, a few sparks, and a four-year-old boy sitting on the living room carpet bellowing a cry that could be heard around the world. Needless to say, I never again licked an electric race car track!

The Theory

I have a theory. I believe that life-changing, energizing experience never would have taken place had the power cord not been plugged in.

Do you agree? Think of a car. A car can have a new engine, gas in the tank, good tires, and a key in the ignition; but all this is useless without a battery. The power source has to be there to make it run.

It's the same with an electric guitar. Recently I was in the recording studio with "Star Search" winner David Slater to co-produce a song for a young man named Jon Evans Conley. Every time I'm around this kid I become more amazed at his ability to play a guitar. Move over Eddie Van Halen! But my theory applies here as well. No matter how good Jon can play an electric guitar, no sound will bless the ears of listeners until the power cord of the amp is plugged in.

One last example is that of a computer. Computers are marvelous inventions that have transformed every area of life — work, school and play. The capabilities of a computer are almost limitless. But a computer is just a worthless pile of metal and plastic if it is not plugged into its power source.

Application

Your life mirrors the examples given in this chapter. Like the electric race car track, you can experience a constant flow of energizing electricity when you plug in to the power. Like the car, it's possible for you to run smoothly and powerfully when you have a power source. Like an electric guitar, your life can produce beautiful music for many to hear when you plug in the power cord. Like a computer, you have almost limitless capabilities to do incredible things on this earth, but only when you plug in to the power.

What or whom is this power source? "Christ the power of God and the wisdom of God. For the foolishness of God is wiser than man's wisdom, and the weakness of God is stronger than man's strength."[1] When you make the decision to plug in to the power of Jesus Christ, you will become a different person. His power will be shared with you. "For God did not give us a spirit of timidity, but a spirit of power, of love and of self-discipline."[2]

So what are you waiting for? Grab that power cord, and focus your eyes on the power source. "Be strong in the Lord and in his mighty power,"[3] and PLUG IN TO THE POWER!

Process and Output

1. In the context of Jesus being tried before Pilate, read John 19:8-11. Who had the greater power?

Where does this power originate?

What does this teach you about power in the world today?

2. Have you ever seen lightning strike a transformer on a telephone pole? Smoke emerges with a loud pop. Then the lights go off in near-by houses. Why? Because the transformer is responsible for supplying electricity to those who live around it. When it goes down, so does the power supply.

God is much like a transformer. He contains power. He gives power. He is the power source. God spoke, and the universe came into existence. God continued creating as He gave to humanity His Word, the Bible. This, also, came to us through God's power and it contains power for us (like the transformer). Romans 1:16 teaches, "I am not ashamed of the gospel, because it is the power of God for the salvation of everyone who believes." God pours out His power onto our spiritual needs. He is our power source. He is our transformer.

Draw a picture that comes to mind when you think of God's eternal power (see Romans 1:20 and Jude 25).

3. Some teenagers think they are too weak spiritually to be Christians. They're afraid they can't live up to the standards they perceive Christians should have. Others are physically weak or "socially lame," and the concept of strength and power seems foreign to them. The apostle Paul could have easily fit into one or both of these categories. But read what he wrote in 2 Corinthians 12:7-10. Write your reaction to the passage:

4. Study carefully Ephesians 1:15-23 and Colossians 1:9-14. Write from memory as many characteristics of the power of God as you can.

example: <u>strengthens my patience</u>   _____

                  _____   _____

                  _____   _____

                  _____   _____

ENDNOTES

1. 1 Corinthians 1:24b-25.
2. 2 Timothy 1:7.
3. Ephesians 6:10.

2 Friday the 13th — the Real Version

Power is associated with light. Therefore, logic concludes that the lack of power is associated with darkness. Have you ever been sitting in the house on a stormy night, watching television, when a power failure happens? Lights go out, the television picture fades, and the hum of the air conditioner dies. Darkness and silence. You sit wide-eyed. The first thought that comes to your mind is, "Where's the flashlight?"

Few of us like constant darkness. We want to be in the light. Something sinister is associated with darkness. That thought brings us to our text for this chapter. The context is the crucifixion of Jesus. Mark 15:33-39 reports:

> At the sixth hour darkness came over the whole land until the ninth hour. And at the ninth hour Jesus cried out in a loud voice, "Eloi, Eloi, lama sabachthani?" — which means, "My God, my God, why have you forsaken me?" When some of those standing near heard this, they said, "Listen, he's calling Elijah." One man ran, filled a sponge with wine vinegar, put it on a stick, and offered it to Jesus to drink. "Now leave him alone. Let's see if Elijah comes to take him down," he said. With a loud cry, Jesus breathed his last. The curtain of the temple was torn in two from top to bottom. And when the centurion, who stood there in front of Jesus, heard his cry and saw how he died, he said, "Surely this man was the Son of God!"

Did you notice anything unusual about that text? Look again at the opening verse: "At the sixth hour, **darkness** came over the whole land until the ninth hour" (emphasis added). According to Jewish time, the sixth hour was noon. The darkness lasted from noon to 3 p.m.

Suppose you and your family go to the park for a picnic lunch. It's noon, and the sun is painting a cloudless blue sky. All of a sudden, as if someone flipped a light switch in the heavens, the sky turns black. You can barely see the potato chip on your plate. The whole area is enveloped by an eerie darkness. Would you think anything about it? Would you be a little curious? Or would you do as I would and almost swallow your tongue?

> *Contrary to the polished, gold-plated emphasis most people place on Golgotha today, the cross of Christ actually portrays the ugliness of sin.*

I want you to understand that the Friday in A.D. 33[1] when Jesus was crucified was no normal Friday! It was a day of unusual events. It seemed a day of disaster, because evidently the Devil had won. Jesus Christ, the Son of God, was dying on a cross. Satan's forces cheered. Demons rejoiced. Darkness ruled. It seemed that God's power had been unplugged.

Dark Shadows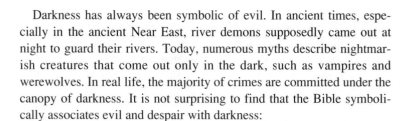

Darkness has always been symbolic of evil. In ancient times, especially in the ancient Near East, river demons supposedly came out at night to guard their rivers. Today, numerous myths describe nightmarish creatures that come out only in the dark, such as vampires and werewolves. In real life, the majority of crimes are committed under the canopy of darkness. It is not surprising to find that the Bible symbolically associates evil and despair with darkness:

Proverbs 2:12-13

Wicked men walk in *dark* ways.

Isaiah 50:3

Distress and *darkness* will be on the children of Israel if they do not follow God.

Matthew 8:12; 22:13; and 25:30

Hell is described as outer *darkness*.

John 8:12

Those who follow Jesus do not walk in *darkness*.

John 12:46

Those who believe in Jesus should not continue in *darkness*.

Acts 26:18

One should turn from *darkness*.

Romans 13:12

One should cast off *darkness*.

2 Corinthians 6:14

Darkness and light have no union.

Ephesians 5:11

Darkness consists of unfruitful works.

Ephesians 6:12

Darkness has rulers (reference to Satan).

Colossians 1:13

God has rescued those who believe from the power of *darkness*.

1 Peter 2:9

God calls us out of *darkness*.

1 John 1:5

God is light, in Him there is no *darkness*.

1 John 1:6

If we have fellowship with Jesus, we cannot walk in the *darkness*.

Are you surprised that the Bible so often uses the metaphor of darkness? God, in His infinite wisdom, knows how to communicate a point to us! Are you scared of the dark? Do you still sleep with a Mickey Mouse night light or a teddy bear? How many times in the last month did you check your closet before going to bed?

Personally, I don't mind being at home alone during the daytime. But if it's nighttime, it's a different story. I turn on every light in the house, look under each bed, check every closet, and even peep behind the shower curtain. I don't know what I'll do if I ever find someone peeping back! Maybe this uneasiness was caused by a television show I watched when I was a kid. One of the main characters was a vampire named Barnabas Collins. He was always hiding in the shadows waiting on his next victim. Can you guess the name of the show? "Dark Shadows."

Application

Darkness has always been the partner of evil. That Friday afternoon in A.D. 33 was no exception. It was a dreary afternoon, full of darkness and despair. It seemed that the Devil had won. Can't you just hear him cackling to his demons: "We have won! He's dead! The Son is down! Now where is God's power?" And for a brief period in history, he was right. The Son was separated from the life-giving power of the Father. Jesus had to bear the sins of the whole world with no help or relief from anyone. He was tumbling through the deep dark pits of hell in what looked like defeat by a slimy, scandalous Satan.

As we look at it, the overall picture is one of doom and despair. Demons rejoicing. Rocks crying out. The world holding its breath. Sin soaring through the air. For you see, contrary to the polished, gold-plated emphasis most people place on Golgotha today, the cross of Christ actually portrays the ugliness of sin.

It was no normal Friday. It was "Friday the thirteenth" — the real version. Darkness rained. Darkness reigned. The sun was down. The Son was down. Had the power really been unplugged?

Process and Output

1. Describe the darkest event of your life:

Place a check mark by the word that best defines your feelings when you think of this dark experience:

happy	_____	overjoyed	_____
scared	_____	terrified	_____
calm	_____	unemotional	_____
other	_____	*(write the word)*	

2. What do you consider to be the darkest experience recorded in the Bible?

What makes it so "dark"?

3. Reread the text of Mark 15:33-39, and then draw a picture of what you see:

4. React to the following sentence taken from this chapter: "Contrary to the polished, gold-plated emphasis most place on Golgotha today, the cross of Christ actually portrays the ugliness of sin."

ENDNOTES

1. The traditional dating for the life of Jesus placed the crucifixion in A.D. 33. Recent scholarship has identified changes in calendaring systems that might produce an alternative date of A.D. 30.

3 The Empty Bird Cage

The Friday in A.D. 33 when Jesus was crucified was a day of darkness and despair. Friday the thirteenth the real version was doomsday. But the following Sunday was the Son's day. As the early morning rays of golden sunlight kissed the dawning sky, a remarkable event took place that changed the course of history forever. It's reported in Mark 16:1-6:

> When the Sabbath was over, Mary Magdalene, Mary the mother of James, and Salome bought spices so that they might go to anoint Jesus' body. Very early on the first day of the week, just after sunrise, they were on their way to the tomb and they asked each other, "Who will roll the stone away from the entrance of the tomb?"
>
> But when they looked up, they saw that the stone, which was very large, had been rolled away. As they entered the tomb, they saw a young man dressed in a white robe sitting on the right side, and they were alarmed.
>
> "Don't be alarmed," he said. "You are looking for Jesus the Nazarene, who was crucified. He has risen!"

Jesus broke forth from that dark, despairing tomb. At that moment He seized victory from the clutches of Satan. Jesus had conquered sin and death! The sun was out. The Son was out!

The Impact of the Resurrection

One day a Christian was walking through an art gallery in Glasgow, Scotland. He came upon a small boy who was gazing intently at a painting of the crucifixion. After watching him for a moment, the man laid a hand on the boy's shoulder and said, "Young man, what is this picture of?"

"Why, sir," said the boy, "don't you know? It is our Lord dying on the cross. He's bearing our sins."

The man, pleased with the boy's answer, patted him on the head and said, "That's right, son." He then walked on, looking at other paintings in the gallery.

Suddenly, the man felt a tug on his sleeve. "Pardon me, sir," the boy said. "I forgot one thing. He's not dead anymore. He's alive!"

The resurrection of Jesus Christ is the ultimate reason for Christians to rejoice. For too long, many Christians have been focusing their gaze only on the cross. It's time we leap with joy in front of the empty tomb! Anybody could die on a cross. Thousands did. But only one rose from the grave.

To preach "Jesus Christ and him crucified"[1] is vital. The message of Christ must always contain the message of the cross. My co-worker Dr. John Cannon says, "We must never be guilty of preaching a Christless cross or a crossless Christ!" But as John would agree, the teaching of the cross is only half the message. There's another side to the coin. "I want to know Christ and the power of his resurrection."[2] Without the resurrection, the death of Jesus on the cross would have been in vain. The atoning sacrifice came on the cross. The conquering power came through the resurrection.

A Lesson from a Bird Cage

Dr. S.D. Gordon, a well-known Boston preacher and author from years past, illustrated this point well one Sunday morning for his congregation. He stepped onto the podium and placed a beat-up, rusted bird cage beside the pulpit, in full view of the audience. He then began to relate how that he had met a grimy little boy in a back ally the week before. The boy was walking along and carrying the old bird cage. Inside the cage were several birds. Dr. Gordon stopped the boy and asked, "Son, what are you going to do with those birds?"

The little boy replied, "I'm gonna play with them and have fun with them."

"You can't do that forever. You will finally get tired of playing with the birds. What are you going to do with them then?" said Dr. Gordon.

"Well, I haven't really thought about that. I guess I'll feed them to my cat. He likes birds!"

> *For too long, many Christians have been focusing their gaze only on the cross. It's time we leap for joy in front of the empty tomb!*

Dr. Gordon was a compassionate man, and he didn't like the idea of a cat eating those poor, defenseless birds. He said to the boy, "How much do you want for those birds?"

The boy was surprised and responded, "Sir, you don't want these birds. They're just ugly field birds. They carry diseases. They can't even sing. They're not good for anything. You don't want these birds."

"How much?" Dr. Gordon persisted.

The grimy little fellow wrinkled his forehead, stroked his chin and finally said, "Two dollars!"

To his surprise, Dr. Gordon reached into his back pocket, pulled out his wallet, and revealed two new, crisp one-dollar bills. The little fellow snatched the money away from Dr. Gordon, handed him the bird cage, and disappeared like a flash down the alley. The compassionate Dr. Gordon then bent down between the towering brick walls of that back ally, opened the door of the bird cage, and began gently tapping on the exterior of the rusted cage until each little bird had gone out the door and flown to freedom.

Having accounted for the empty cage beside his pulpit, Dr. Gordon went on to tell what at first seemed to be a totally different story. The story was about a conversation Jesus and the Devil could have once had.

Jesus came upon the Devil one day. It appeared that Satan had trapped a world full of people in a cage. "What are you going to do with those people?" Jesus asked.

"Well, I'm going to play with them. I'm going to make them cheat, lie, gossip, steal, murder, and commit adultery. I'm just going to have fun with them," replied the Devil.

Jesus responded, "You can't do that forever. You will finally get tired of it. What are you going to do then?"

"I haven't really thought of that," said the Devil. "I guess I'll just condemn them. That's what I'll do. I'll condemn them!"

"How much do you want for them?" asked Jesus.

"You don't want these people," the Devil replied. "They're ugly. They're mean. They carry diseases. Why, they would just spit on you, mock you, whip you, and finally kill you. You don't want these people."

But Jesus persisted, "How much?"

The Devil wrinkled his forehead, stroked his chin and finally said, "All your tears, and all your blood!"

So Jesus paid the price (on the cross), opened the door (in His resurrection), and you and I flew to freedom.

Application

Freedom is a priceless gift. In my office is a small piece of the Berlin wall. The magnificent breakdown of that wall in 1989 showed the entire world that freedom is attainable. The young Chinese student standing in front of the tank brigade at Tiananmen Square was a statement to the entire world that freedom is precious enough to die for.

And that's exactly what Jesus did. Jesus loves freedom — not a freedom that allows us to fly in any direction we want, but rather a freedom that offers us the liberty to be holy and righteous. A freedom from the shackles of sin and eternal death, ironically releasing us to become "slaves to God."[3]

Jesus loves our freedom so much that He went to the cross. And it was not a nail that held Him to the rugged wood; love kept Him there. He completed His mission of *agape*[4] when He emerged from that damp, dark, musty tomb on Sunday morning. Even more than my little piece of the Berlin wall, I would love to have a piece of that stone that was rolled back in A.D. 33, for it announces to the world that freedom is available for eternity.

Though it appeared that the power had been unplugged as darkness enveloped the cross, seeing the open tomb proclaims that the power is still very much plugged in. And every morning when the sun rises in the east, we're reminded of that special morning when not only the sun rose, but the Son rose. As a result, His power, His light, and His freedom can be experienced by everyone who plugs in to His power.

Process and Output

1. What comes to mind when you read the words "power of His resurrection" in Philippians 3:10?

2. List five things you can find in nature that remind you of the resurrection of Jesus Christ (example: an empty cocoon):
a.)
b.)
c.)
d.)
e.)

3. Draw a picture of the freedom offered to you by the resurrection (whatever comes to mind):

4. Make a list of all the places you might see a cross today (on a necklace, on a church building, etc.):

Keep a record for one week of how many crosses you see in the places listed above.   Total _____ .

Compare this number to the number of empty tombs you've seen represented in similar places (on a necklace, etc.) over the past year. What does this tell you about the theology of religious people in general? Write your feelings in the space below:

Special note: If you have difficulty accepting the resurrection of Jesus Christ as a historical event, consider reading the book *The Resurrection Factor* by Josh McDowell.

ENDNOTES

1. 1 Corinthians 2:2; 1:23.
2. Philippians 3:10. See also Romans 8:34.
3. Romans 6:22; see verses 20-23.
4. Greek word for the strongest and most intimate level of love known to humanity.

4 The Ultimate Electric Outlet

"Go find a wife, " Isaac said to his son Jacob. So Jacob loaded his camel and headed out to find the woman of his dreams. What would she be like — good looking, intelligent, have a good sense of humor, a hard worker or a good homemaker?

Jacob traveled east toward the land of his ancestors. His search intensified when he reached Paddan Aram. He was hot and thirsty, and his camel needed a drink. As Genesis 29:2-3 reports,

> There he saw a well in the field, with three flocks of sheep lying near it because the flocks were watered from that well. The stone over the mouth of the well was large. When all the flocks were gathered there, the shepherds would roll the stone away from the well's mouth and water the sheep. Then they would return the stone to its place over the mouth of the well.

That must have been a big rock. Jacob asked the shepherds why they didn't go ahead and water their sheep. Their reply was that they couldn't move the stone until all the shepherds were gathered to lend a hand. Now enters the female:

> While he (Jacob) was still talking with them, Rachel came with her father's sheep, for she was a shepherdess. When Jacob saw Rachel, daughter of Laban, his mother's brother, and Laban's sheep, his eyes bulged out of his head, his heart began pounding, and the palms of his hands began to sweat profusely!

Wait a minute! That's not what Genesis 29:9-10 says! But I imagine Jacob's first encounter with Rachel would come very close to fitting that description. The text does say, "When Jacob saw Rachel ... he went over and rolled the stone away from the mouth of the well and watered his uncle's sheep" (v. 10). What a show-off! Jacob was being Mr. Macho. He was flexing his biceps. He didn't wait on the other shepherds. He wanted to win the heart of this young beauty by demonstrating his manliness. And it worked. The very next verse in Genesis says he kissed her! He even ended up marrying her. What a love story!

The Hopeless Romantic

You may be sighing with envy after reading that story. Maybe no one has ever carried your school books, sent you roses, or left a "secret admirer" note in your locker. Your mailbox may be empty every Valentine's Day. You may be totally convinced that Cupid has overlooked you ... no one has ever tried to impress you by rolling a large stone just for you. If that's what you believe, you had better think again!

At 9 a.m. on a Friday, they crucified Jesus. At 3 p.m., Jesus "cried out again in a loud voice, [and] he gave up his spirit."[1] As the sun set that Friday afternoon, Jesus' body was placed inside a tomb, and a man named Joseph of Arimathea "rolled a big stone in front of the entrance to the tomb and went away."[2] Three days later,

> When the Sabbath was over, Mary Magdalene, Mary the mother of James, and Salome bought spices so that they might go to anoint Jesus' body. Very early on the first day of the week, just after sunrise, they were on their way to the tomb and they asked each other, "Who will roll the stone away from the entrance of the tomb?" But when they looked up, they saw that the stone, which was very large, had been rolled away.[3]

So there you have it! From hopeless romantic to hopeful romantic in one instant. Someone has attempted to win your heart. Someone has moved a big rock just for you. Someone has tried to impress you with His power. And that someone is the Lord of the universe!

The Ultimate Electric Outlet

Suppose you have a sweetheart. One evening that sweetheart takes you to the most expensive restaurant in town. The waiter seems to recognize your date and leads you to a cozy corner table where two candles have already been lit. Romantic music is playing softly in the background. You order and eat a superb meal, being careful not to spill anything on your best outfit. After dinner, the waiter comes to take your plate away. You just happen to notice that the waiter is looking at your sweetheart and nodding subtly. Something is up! A couple of minutes pass. Your sweetheart is beginning to fidget nervously. Your favorite song begins to play. Your hands begin to perspire.

> *Jesus has gone to great lengths to win your heart. He has offered you a gift unparalleled in value.*

Then it happens. The waiter returns, smiling from ear to ear, and places a small wrapped gift on the table in front of you. You look at the gift and then at your sweetheart, whose left eye is beginning to twitch. You look down at the gift and read the tag: "If every time I thought of you a drop of water evaporated, the oceans would be empty." WOW! Could it be? Your favorite song is now on its second verse — you know the one. You attempt to speak, but your sweetheart stops you by touching a finger to your lips. "Don't say anything," he says. "Just cherish the moment. I've been saving up for a year now so that I might give this to you. It means everything in the world to me. I hope it means as much to you."

Your shaking hands begin to unwrap the paper clumsily. Inside is a blue velvet jewelry box with the words "Saks Fifth Avenue" inscribed in gold. You realize your lips are break dancing on each other. You know what's in the box. You have dreamed about this moment time after time and now it's really happening! Two heartbeats pound out a rapid rhythm at a corner table in the restaurant. The last verse of your song begins. You place your left thumb and index finger around the top of the box. You look down at the box, take a deep breath, and you open it. Silence. Pause. Your eyes widen. More silence. More pause. There, in the velvet box resting within your hand, is ... an electric outlet.

You are speechless. The thought occurs to you that this might be a joke. But the thought quickly goes away when you look up and see the genuine sincerity on your sweetheart's face. You know you need to say something, so you begin to grapple for words. You finally sputter out, "Uh, it's, uh, the most beautiful electric outlet I've ever been given."

Sound like a pretty absurd story? But, think again. You have been given an electric outlet. The gift is before your eyes at this very moment. But this is no ordinary electric outlet. It's the ultimate electric outlet. It contains the power to work incredible wonders in your life. It was given to you by the Father through Jesus, His Son, unveiled from within the velvet box of the tomb. "And if the Spirit of him who raised Jesus from the dead is living in you, he who raised Christ from the dead will also give life to your mortal bodies through his Spirit, who lives in you."[4]

Application

This ultimate electric outlet has the power to forgive your sins. It has the power to promise you eternal life with God. It automatically gets you adopted into the mightiest family of all God's family. You become an heir of all God has — everything!

This electric outlet has the power to cause you to praise God when tribulation and trouble knock at your door, because you understand that these will develop perseverance within your character.[5] It offers a peace and a joy that nothing in the universe can compare to.[6] But it must be plugged in to.

To decide not to accept this beautiful gift of love means to live in total darkness for eternity. It would be similar to buying a computer, setting it up on your desk, familiarizing yourself with the operator's manual, and then never plugging it in.

Jesus has gone to great lengths to win your heart. He has offered you a gift unparalleled in value. There are no fine-print clauses. There are no gimmicks. All you have to do is to accept the gift and say yes to the marriage proposal of Jesus.

Just like a in a marriage of husband and wife, you must make a verbal commitment to Jesus so that the world knows your intentions. You can then consummate that marriage in the beautiful act of baptism. You are then joined with Jesus and entitled to wear His name — Christian. A wedding gift is given to you by the Father — the gift of the Holy Spirit.

This is what it means to plug in to the power! Will you?

Process and Output

1. What is your favorite romantic scene from all the movies you've watched?

2. List three romantic scenes from the Bible:
   a.)
   b.)
   c.)

3. You have just personally received a gift from Jesus. It's the ultimate electric outlet described in this chapter. Write a love letter to Jesus in response to this gift:

Dear Jesus,

_____

_____

_____

_____

_____

_____

_____

_____

_____

_____

_____

                                        All My Love Forever,

                                        _____

4. In the two columns below, list all of the disadvantages of plugging in to the power of Jesus Christ, and then all of the advantages:

DISADVANTAGES	ADVANTAGES

ENDNOTES

1. Matthew 27:50
2. Matthew 27:60
3. Mark 16:1-4
4. Romans 8:11
5. See James 1:2-3
6. See Ephesians 1:3-8

Section 2
Mark 12:28-30

Load God's Program

CLICK
CLICK

5 You Have to Have a Program

"Zap!" Good choice. So now you're plugged in to God's power. Your computer is humming and ready for step number two — programming. A computer, even though it is plugged in to the power source, can't do anything without a set of instructions — a program. You'll have to decide which program to load. Word processing? Database? Spreadsheet? Graphics? Remember, the computer can only operate according to the program you decide to load. So what will it be? Decisions, decisions, decisions.

Daily Decisions

Decisions are not new to you. Did you realize that every day you make hundreds of decisions? This morning, when you got up, you decided which clothes you were going to wear. "Let's see, will it be the pre-washed jeans, the stone-washed jeans, or the jeans that look like they got caught in the lawn mower?" You also made a decision about what to eat for breakfast, how to fix your hair, and which pair of shoes to wear.

You decided to brush your teeth or to leave the sausage chunk behind your right molar for a mid-morning snack. You decided whether or not to wear deodorant. Now, at this point I think it's important for you to understand something. Many of the daily decisions you make will affect other people. And believe me, if you chose not to brush your teeth or put on deodorant this morning, you are affecting other people!

Desiring to Know

Because of the impact decisions have on me, as well as on others, I sometimes find myself wishing for a crystal ball. I wish I could see the outcome of certain decisions before I make them. Wouldn't it be great if there was a computer program that would foretell the future and portray on the screen the outcome of each decision I make? But there's no such program. Crystal balls don't work. Yet I continue to live with a strong desire to know the outcome of each decision I face.

Let's focus on the word "desire" in the previous sentence. Webster defines the word as "to long for; to wish intensely for." A desire is an intense emotional feeling that causes one to wish for or search for answers. Suppose you are chosen to be on "The Price Is Right." Bob Barker walks up to you and says, "There's a red Corvette that I want to give away. If you can select the correct price from these five prices on the board, you will be driving home in a brand new car. You get one try." Would you desire to know which of those five prices is correct? You bet!

> *According to Jesus, there is an ultimate decision that leads to an ultimate outcome — loving God with all your heart, soul, mind and strength.*

Suppose you run for a student council office. The votes are cast on Friday but the results will not be revealed until Monday. Are you going to be anxious all weekend because of your desire to know the outcome of the election? More than likely.

Maybe you desire to know if that certain boy or girl likes you. You develop a plan that includes your best friend who is supposed to go and strike up a conversation with that person. During the conversation, your best friend is to casually mention your name and then watch for the reaction on the other person's face. You hide at your locker, awaiting the verdict. Or maybe you do like some "highly mature" teenagers I know. They write a note and send it to the person: "I like you. Do you like me? Circle one: Yes or No."

I remember when I first had the desire to know what kissing was like. One morning, at the beginning of my second grade year, I was getting ready to go to school. I was wearing tennis shoes and had been scooting my feet on the carpet. I grabbed my schoolbooks and lunch box and headed toward the front door. My mother was holding the door open. As usual, I reached up to kiss her on the cheek. But for some reason, on that particular morning, I decided to kiss my mother on the lips. Not knowing that my shoes had generated some static electricity, my lips were about two inches from my mother's when the sparks flew. Wow!

My desire to know what kissing was like was answered that morning in North Little Rock, Ark. Okay, so it was only my mother. But it was an electrifying experience. I wish I could say the same for some of the desires to know that I currently have in my heart.

Knowing the Ultimate

When I was a little boy, the whole country desired to know if man could walk on the moon. President John F. Kennedy challenged America to put a man on the moon before the decade was over. Space flights began to take place. Success was common. Then, suddenly, on Jan. 27, 1967, a catastrophic fire swept through Apollo 1 on the launchpad. Three astronauts died — Roger Chaffee, Virgil Grissom and Edward White. But that did not kill the pressing desire of the American people. Space flights continued. And at 10:56 p.m. on July 20, 1969, Neil Armstrong stepped into history from the bottom rung of the ladder leading down from Apollo 11's landing craft. He reached out his booted left foot and planted the first human footprint on the moon. Then Armstrong uttered the long-awaited words that are sure to be remembered as long as this earth stands: "That's one small step for a man, one giant leap for mankind."

People seem to have an innate, insatiable desire to know the ultimate in everything. Once we knew what it was like to put a man on the moon, we wanted to go to Mars. We want to know which building is the tallest. What's the fastest car? Where is the largest city? Who is the wealthiest person? We always want to rank things and know which is the best or most important.

It's not surprising, therefore, in view of mankind's unquenchable desire to know the unknown and exceptional, that the question in Mark 12:28 was asked. A teacher of the Law of Moses walked up to Jesus and said, "Of all the commandments [in the Law of Moses], which is the most important?" It's vital to realize that this teacher was not referring just to the Ten Commandments. He was actually referring to the 613 commandments included in the Law of Moses and found in Exodus through Deuteronomy.

You might be tempted to respond by saying that all commandments are equal in the sight of God and that each command is just as important as any other. But that's not how Jesus answered. Jesus had a specific command in mind:

> Love the Lord your God with all your heart and with
> all your soul and with all your mind and with all your
> strength.[1]

According to Jesus, there is an ultimate decision that leads to an ultimate outcome — loving God with all your heart, soul, mind and strength! That's the program Jesus says should control your life.

Application

The output a computer can generate is based on the program that is loaded. The same is true with your life. Your life will outwardly show what you have loaded into it. The program you choose is crucial. It has major consequences.

So, which program will you choose to load into the computer of your soul and base your life upon? The program of the world will take control of your life and grab your priorities. It will command all your heart, soul, mind and strength. That program is based on selfishness and will lead you into loving the trappings and frills of the world. It will also eventually lead you to hell. Let us call this program the WorldImperfect program.

Then there's the program God would have you load to run your life. It's based on love — the kind of love Jesus talked about and showed in His life. God's program will lead you into the joyful life of a Christian. It will take all your heart, soul, mind and strength, but it will eventually lead you to heaven. Let's call this program the *JesusPerfect* program.

Both of these programs are available to you. You have the right and the responsibility to choose which you will load into your soul's computer. Will you load God's program for your life? Remember, your life has to have a program to run on. Which program is your decision? Will it be God or the world? It's a decision of destiny — eternal destiny. Your decision will affect both you and others. So why not base your life on the ultimate program — the *JesusPerfect* program!

Process and Output

1. What's the hardest decision you have ever made?

How did that decision affect you?

2. What one decision in your life affected more people than any other?

3. List the three things you most desire to know.
   a.)

   b.)

   c.)

4. Mark the categories that most grab your attention:
   _____ who is the highest-paid actor
   _____ who is the most beautiful woman alive
   _____ who had two songs in the Top 40
   _____ who has had more #1 hit songs than anyone in history
   _____ who played in the Wimbledon semifinals this year
   _____ who won Wimbledon this year
   _____ who makes $35,000 annually
   _____ who is the richest person alive
   _____ other _____

5. According to Jesus, what is the ultimate thing you should do while living on the earth?

What will the outcome (effect) be if you do this?

ENDNOTES

1. Mark 12:30. Quoting Deuteronomy 6:5.

Everything HEART and Soul

6 Everything Heart and Soul (Part 1)

Geoff Moore sings a song written by David Martin titled "Heart and Soul." The first verse could easily have been sung by Peter, Andrew, James and John as they were fishing on the Sea of Galilee:

I took a walk one day
Right down by the water side
People were standing everywhere
Somebody called my name
Said, son give me what you have
Little or much I don't care
Oh, He wanted everything

I said, I'm giving You ...

Two hands
You can call them Your own
Two feet to lead
Wherever You want them to go
And two eyes to see
The things You want me to know
Said I'm giving You
Everything, everything, everything
Everything heart and soul

The *JesusPerfect* program calls for you to love God with all your heart and with all your soul (Mark 12:30). What does it mean to give everything heart and soul?

The Heart of the Matter

There are two ways to define the word "heart." First, the heart is a large muscle in your chest cavity that pumps your blood and keeps you alive. That is not the heart Jesus is referring to in Mark 12:30. Second, the heart is that part of you that feels. It's the part of you where the emotions rest. It also generates motive and will. If you say "My heart is breaking" or "I love you with all my heart," you are referring to this definition. And it's this definition Jesus has in mind in Mark 12:30.

Just as the muscle called the heart is the center of life for your physical body, the feeling response called the heart is at the center of your spiritual body. It must be programmed to respond to God out of love. And that's the heart of the matter.

Heart to Heart

One of the most incredible experiences of my life took place on March 13, 1989. My wife, Mandy, was pregnant with our first child, Christin. We went that day to the doctor's office, where an ultrasound was to be done to check the baby's heartbeat. I'm writing a journal for my little girl that I'll give her some day, and here is my entry to Christin from that day:

> Today I heard your heartbeat. The nurse rubbed some lotion on your mommie's stomach and placed a small metal device on it. Immediately the room filled with the sound of life — your life. I was in awe! It was as if, for the first time, I really felt you were communicating with us. Mandy cried. I praised God for that heartbeat. Today my prayer for you took a new direction. I now pray that the Lord will take your physical heartbeat and implant it within your soul and that the world will hear your spiritual heartbeat ringing with the message of the true life in Jesus Christ.

Just as I heard that beautiful "tick ... tick ... tick" today, I pray that you will also carry with you the heartbeat of Jesus. It is for that special reason that He is creating you in the warm and cozy womb of your mother. The world will not always be warm and cozy, and there will be some who will not be awed or swayed by your heartbeat. But if you make a difference for only one, a lifetime of living with the heartbeat of Jesus will be worth it. Sleep tight, little one, for soon you will say hello to a bright and lively world.

During the days that followed this beautiful experience, I kept thinking about the rhythm of the heartbeats produced by Mandy and Christin. Mandy's heart was large and strong, about the size of a pear. It produced a steady, firm, rhythmic beat that was as constant as waves in the ocean. And then there was Christin's heartbeat generating from a heart the size of a marble. It produced a not-so-firm, sporadic heartbeat. Even an untrained ear could tell that this little heart still needed some development. It relied on a stronger source to keep it going. And that's when it hit me — if the mother's heart stops, so does the baby's! The child's heart is relying on the mother's heart to keep it alive so that it may grow stronger and develop. They are literally intertwined — heart to heart.

> *If you make a difference for only one, a lifetime of living with the heartbeat of Jesus will be worth it.*

That is precisely the way it is with you and God. Your heart is reliant upon God's heart. You must have His continuous love or your spiritual heart will die. And that continuous love must be returned to God in response. That's the greatest possible action you can take on this earth, because it is in direct response to the greatest command from Jesus. It is one of the vital steps in God's program for your life.

Is your heart beating in unison with God's? Or is your heart quivering its last beat? Have you allowed your heart to grow cold and weak by starving it from the warmth and power of God's love? If so, all hope is not lost. There's something you can do to once again have true life in Jesus Christ. It's time for you to get ...

A Heart Transplant

Her name was Maria and she was eighteen years old. She had lived all her life with a weakening heart muscle. It was only a matter of time before she died. After a heart attack, Maria was taken to the intensive care unit at Illinois Masonic Hospital, where doctors speculated that she had only a few days left to live. Maria had a four-month-old daughter, and she began to accept the fact that she would never enjoy the blessings of watching her daughter grow up.

That's when the unexpected happened. Another teenage girl from the same area suffered a neurological disorder that left her brain dead, but with a healthy heart. The mother of this girl heard about Maria's condition and made a difficult decision. She said to Maria's mother, "I want to donate my daughter's heart so that your daughter can go on living."

Both girls were moved to the University of Illinois Hospital, where the heart transplant took place. The doctors pronounced the transplanted heart "an excellent match," and said that Maria's chances for survival were very good. Only after this entire ordeal did Maria find out that the healthy heart she received had been given by one of her friends from her neighborhood and high school. Maria vowed that one of her first trips, when she returned home from the hospital, would be to visit her friend's mother. "I will try to be just like a daughter to her, because I have part of her daughter living in me." Two separate people sharing one heart.

Application

If your spiritual heart is weak, if it's dying, you need a heart transplant. There is One who is willing to give His heart so that you may live. Two separate beings sharing one heart. His name is Jesus.

Some doctors have studied the death of Jesus in detail. They claim that Jesus died from heart failure as a result of the excruciating experience of the cross. But you and I know what it really was — He gave His heart away! A strong heart that's full of life. And He gave it to you. The question is simple, but the answer has profound consequences: Will you accept the heart of Jesus, and will you give Him your heart full of love for what He has done for you? If your answer is yes, you have begun running the *JesusPerfect* program in your life.

Process and Output

1. How many hours do you spend each day strengthening your:

PHYSICAL	HEART	SPIRITUAL	HEART
Sunday	_____	Sunday	_____
Monday	_____	Monday	_____
Tuesday	_____	Tuesday	_____
Wednesday	_____	Wednesday	_____
Thursday	_____	Thursday	_____
Friday	_____	Friday	_____
Saturday	_____	Saturday	_____
TOTAL HOURS	_____	TOTAL HOURS	_____

2. Reflect on the life that is produced by your physical heart muscle. Try to discover spiritual parallels, and then write a journal entry to God about your insights:

3. Draw a picture of how the "intertwined relationship" between God's heart and your heart should look (whatever comes to mind):

4. Is your heartbeat in unison with God's? Fill in the spiritual heart monitor below with your spiritual heartbeat at the present time:

Spiritual Heart Monitor

God's Heartbeat

Your Heartbeat

7 Everything Heart and Soul (Part 2)

The whip cracked like lightning from the hand of the Roman soldier. The multipronged scourge had satisfied its relentless passion for blood once again. This time it was a woman — a mother of three. Some of the bloodthirsty Romans standing nearby were moved to tears of pity for this woman whose arteries, veins and vital organs were now exposed. Three little children became orphans.

Similar scenes took place often during the period of the Roman persecution against Christians shortly after the time of Jesus. Some of the Christian martyrs displayed such heroism that not a single cry or groan emerged from their lips. Husbands and wives, boyfriends and girlfriends, parents and children were torn from one another and brutally killed within the presence of the other.

And then there were those who were taken to the games. Tens of thousands of Romans would gather in a large coliseum (much like our football stadiums today). There the Christians were brought in and forced to lie on beds of nails. The object of the "game" was to get the Christian to renounce Jesus Christ, take the oath to Caesar, and offer incense. If the Christian did this, he or she would be set free. If not, he or she would be fed to wild animals while the spectators cheered with inhuman delight.

That's where Germanicus enters the picture. He was one of the Christians taken to the arena. It was a time when the Christian community was losing heart in the midst of such extreme persecution. Germanicus was only a teenager. But he loved God more than anything or anybody. As the Roman soldiers led him into the arena, thousands of spectators began to cheer as they watched anxiously for the beast to be released. It was then that they noticed the youthfulness of this boy.

Their chants began to fade. Even the governor, who was present, had pity on the young lad. He tried to persuade Germanicus to renounce Jesus Christ and take the oath to Caesar. But Germanicus stood firm in his commitment to his Lord. He even used force to drag the wild animal toward him as he offered his life in sacrifice to God. Christians everywhere heard about the valiant death of Germanicus and were strengthened by his remarkable portrayal of love for God.

Young Germanicus loved God with all his heart. But his love went beyond just an emotional response. His love seeped into the crevices of his soul, and as a result he gave his life for God — just as God in the form of flesh had done for him. That's the ultimate example of what it means to "love the Lord your God with all your heart and with all your soul."[1] For you see, the word for "soul" in this passage is often also translated "life" throughout the New Testament.[2] The passage might properly be translated, "Love the Lord your God with all your heart and with all your life."

The soul is the life of the human being. The Bible even defines death as the separation of soul and body.[3] So the soul is the "life's breath" of a human being. And your love for God, according to Mark 12:30, must be the type of love that motivates you to serve Him with your whole life, even to the point of giving that life for Him as Germanicus did, if such an act of love is ever necessary.

Fillet of Soul

Many of us live in the materialistic, high-energy society of middle-class America. Each one of us has a soul — a life's breath. Each one of us is offering his life's breath to something. That something should be God, but in many cases it's not. This is especially true among teenagers. A survey was conducted of 290,000 college freshmen. The results typified the priorities of the majority of teens in America. Out of the 290,000 students, 75 percent said that being financially well-off is their top priority. Belief in God? Certainly. But money comes before God. To them, money and power offer more peace and contentment than God can ever offer.

As a result of this type of attitude, the soul of these teenagers has been filleted into two pieces. One piece, the larger one, is given to the great god in life (money, power, etc.). The other fillet, the smaller one, is offered to the lesser God (the God of the universe).

Do you fit within this description? Have you filleted your soul into pieces and swallowed hook, line and sinker the bait of the materialistic world? Maybe not. Maybe money or power are not a temptation to you. But is it possible that other things could have become your great god? Sports? Cheerleading? Drill team? Grades? Drama? Cars? Dating? Sex? Friends? Clothes? Music? Movies? Work? God has said part of your soul won't do. He wants it all.

> *His love seeped into the crevices of his soul, and as a result he gave his life for God just as God in the form of flesh had done for him.*

She was fourteen years old. Her hair was long and blonde. She easily could have graced the cover of *Seventeen* magazine. She had a gentle disposition and a beautiful smile. Mandy and I began the Bible study with her at our dining room table. Week after week, we met to discuss God and His plan for mankind. Finally she yielded her life to God and was baptized into Christ.

Never before had I seen any person so excited about living for the Lord. Within three months, she had converted four of her friends. Within eighteen months of her own conversion, twenty-two teenagers from that little, rural Arkansas community were brought to the Lord by this young girl. To say that she loved the Lord God with all her heart and soul would be the understatement of the decade!

Then something happened. It took several weeks for me to notice it, but I finally realized Lasonya didn't have the same "fire" in her life that she had previously portrayed. She seemed to be burning out. She started missing worship assemblies. She missed a few Tuesday night Bible studies. She made it to only a few of the youth group activities. She seldom spoke up in group discussions. Her smile was fading. Even her disposition had changed. This went on for several months. Then she was gone.

Visits were made. Cards were sent. Calls were abundant. But no response. Prayers continued. Then one day, I heard a knock on my office door. I opened it to see Lasonya holding an envelope in her hand. In the envelope was the following letter that she had written to the youth group:

Everyone,

There is so much I want to say. I guess I will start by saying hi. I want to say that I haven't stopped loving the Lord. It's just that I've been so confused lately. I'm taking one day at a time. I got so involved with everything around me that I forgot everything that was important in my life — my relationship with God. But I thought about it, and I didn't have to think too hard, that "what is life without the Lord?" and I concluded that without the Lord, life is nothing! So I have been a "walking nothing" for a couple of months. I want to tell you all something. You may let it go in one ear and out the other, but when you get the Lord out of your life, and you don't really want to, you better take hold of Jesus and have faith more than you ever have before, because if you don't, it's going to get easier and easier to let go of Him completely. And that's something you don't want to do. I know I'm not a good example for everyone to follow, but I'm trying my hardest. And with Jesus' help, I know I'll make it!

Love Every One of You,
Lasonya

One sentence in her letter sums up the major problem so many teens face in responding to the command of Jesus in Mark 12:30 to "love God with all of your soul [life]." It's this sentence found in the middle of the letter: "I got so involved with everything around me that I forgot everything that was important in my life — my relationship with God." Lasonya had not become a bad person. She didn't fall prey to devil worship, drugs or alcohol. She wasn't having sex. She wasn't even tempted by money or power. She simply became too focused on her schoolwork, cheerleading and social clubs. These things became her gods. And the same scene is taking place every day with teenagers all across America. Only the names and places are different.

Application

There are thousands of Lasonyas, young people who know that Jesus wants them to love Him with their entire soul, not just a tiny fillet of soul. They are kids who have the heart of a Christian and who feel the emotional tie to God, but who just can't seem to keep God first, above everything and everyone else. It's almost like they have begun loading God's program for their life, but they get sidetracked and fail to complete the installation process.

Satan has his army. Some of his soldiers are dressed in armor that's ugly and repulsive. Some sins are obvious. But some of his soldiers carry beautiful weapons. They may not look like weapons. Many aren't even sinful until they take the place of God.

When you choose to become a Christian, you step onto the battle field. You pick up your weapons and go through the battle of your life attempting to deflect the sinful spears of the Devil as he attempts to knock God off the throne of your heart. How do you do it? I think Jesus had this question in mind in the last part of the greatest commandment recorded in Mark 12:30: "Love the Lord your God ... with all of your mind and all of your strength." It is to these two characteristics that we turn our attention in the next two chapters, as we continue to load the *JesusPerfect* program. Keep those reading glasses on!

Process and Output

1. When you read about Christian martyrs such as young Germanicus, how does it make you feel about your own sacrifices of self?

2. Read the following passages, and then read them again. The second time through, replace the word soul with the word life.

    Mark 12:30
    Matthew 16:26
    3 John 2

Now read the following passages and do the same by replacing the word life with the word soul.

    Matthew 20:28   John 10:14-15, 17
    Mark 8:35   John 13:37-38
    Luke 12:22-23   John 15:13

3. Of the following items, check four that most demand your time and energy:

    _____ homework   _____ girlfriend/boyfriend
    _____ sports   _____ cheerleading
    _____ band   _____ dating
    _____ work   _____ drill team
    _____ drama   _____ music
    _____ friends   _____ clubs (civic, school, etc.)
    _____ television   _____ movies
                              _____ other (name: _____)

4. Go back and reread the letter from Lasonya. Then write a response giving her advice about her problem.

Dear Lasonya,

In Christian Love,

Signed: _____

ENDNOTES

1. Mark 12:30.
2. Matthew 20:28; Mark 8:35; Luke 12:22-23; John 10:14-15, 17; 13:37-38; 15:13.
3. Matthew 10:28

8 Brainwashing

Grenades and missiles rip buildings and people. Homes are scarred by tanks and fighter bomber raids. Mortars and machine guns have taken their deadly toll. Pistols. Rifles. Automatic weapons. The difference between life and death is the squeeze of a trigger or the shouting of a command to open fire. These have been daily realities for those who live in war zones from the Middle East to the former Yugoslavia. Suppose you lived in such a place. Would you be afraid? Would the cries of the dying pierce your heart? Or would you grow accustomed to the sounds?

There's another war zone. No machine guns. No fighter-bombers screaming in the night. No open warfare in the streets. In this war zone, the buildings are unscarred. The people are beautiful. The air is free of the smell of death. Yet people are dying.

Satan is waging all-out war. His intention is to kill eternally. It's a war without guns. But his weapons are even more sophisticated and deadly — thoughts, temptations, hatred, an occasional evil companion, lusts, greed, apathy, prejudice, activities to block out your view of the Lord.

War. Death. Eternal death. Can you hear the sounds of battle? Can you hear the screams of the dying? You can if you listen, really listen. It's all out war.[1] There is no neutrality.[2] Whose side are you on?[3]

The above four paragraphs come from my good friend Robert Brady. He is correct in drawing attention to the spiritual warfare that envelops us.

You may have read some of Frank Peretti's writings on the same subject.[4] What it all means is that you need help from a Higher Power in order to defeat Satan and program your life in the right way. That help is offered by God. Your response should be to plug in to that power (as we discussed in Section 1). That power will enable you to "love the Lord your God with all your heart and with all your soul and with all your mind and with all your strength."[5] We have already defined what it means to love God with heart and soul. But what does Jesus mean when He says to love God "with all your mind"?

The Million Dollar Camera

The mind is the seat of the intellect. People sometimes use the word "brain" when referring to the mind. With it you do your homework. Scientists make great discoveries by using their minds. With the mind a toddler learns to talk. And with your mind you should study God's message to you revealed through the Bible and even through nature itself.

Every day, you and I should take full advantage of the opportunities we have to learn more about God and His will for our lives. Every week, we should benefit from the Bible classes offered at our home congregations. This is part of loving God with all the mind. If you choose not to do this, it's similar to choosing not to eat. And you know that if you don't eat, you'll die. You probably work hard at keeping your physical body in good shape. You eat the right food. You exercise. And whenever your picture is taken, you study it carefully to evaluate how you look.

> *Personally, I'm glad that I don't have to wash my physical brain. But I do have a responsibility to keep my spiritual brain, my mind, clean.*

Suppose a very intelligent scientist (who was using his mind) invented a special $1 million camera. This camera is no ordinary camera. It takes a picture of your physical body, but as the film develops, you discover that it is revealing your mind! What does your picture look like? Is it a well-built, properly fed mass of toned spiritual muscle? Or does the picture reveal a dirty, malnourished lump that's withering away? If you don't like what you see, maybe you need a good brainwashing!

Brainwashing

Suppose you could twist your ears to a point that the top of your skull is loosened. You "pop the lid" and set your hair on the table beside you. Then you reach inside your head, pull out your brain, and wash it just as you do the rest of your body. Grotesque thought, isn't it?

Personally, I'm glad I don't have to wash my physical brain. But I do have a responsibility to keep my spiritual brain, my mind, clean. As Romans 12:2 teaches, "Do not conform any longer to the pattern of this world, but be changed by the renewal of your minds."[6] If your spiritual snapshot looks weak, you had better start doing some brainwashing. Actually, you don't administer the washing. God does! Notice that the verse above says, "be changed." But you do have an active part in this renewal process. Read these verses from Ephesians, and then answer the questions that follow:

> You were taught, with regard to your former way of life, to put off your old self, which is being corrupted by its deceitful desires; to be made new in the attitude of your minds; and to put on the new self, created to be like God in true righteousness and holiness.[7]

1. Are the movies I watch helping me to renew my mind in righteousness and holiness?

2. Does the music I listen to help me to develop a righteous and holy attitude?

3. Are the magazines and books I read contributing to the spiritual wholesomeness of my mind?

4. Do the conversations I have with my friends always consist of pure words and thoughts?

5. Am I feeding my mind a nutritious meal from God's Word every day?

6. Do my actions around non-Christians portray the likeness of God?

If you cannot answer yes to all those questions, you need to schedule a spiritual brainwashing. The sooner the better! The longer you wait, the more set in your ways your mind will become. It's much like the captain of a naval ship on patrol in the Atlantic during World War II. He noticed a strange light shining through the fog. It appeared to be on a direct collision course with his ship. "Signal that ship: 'We are on a collision course, advise you change course twenty degrees' " the captain said.

The reply came back, "Advisable for you to change course twenty degrees."

Indignant, the captain responded, "I'm a captain, change course twenty degrees."

The reply came back, "I'm a seaman second-class. You had better change course twenty degrees."

This time, the captain's voice was filled with anger and it rang of combat, "I'm a battleship. Change course twenty degrees."

The response of flashing light was brief but understood, "I'm a lighthouse."

The captain quickly changed his course!

If you discover you are headed toward dangerous ground spiritually, shouldn't you change your course? If your snapshot looks weak, shouldn't you "be made new in the attitude of your mind; and ... put on the new self, created to be like God in true righteousness and holiness"?[8] If you discover you have a semi-healthy spiritual body but one that could use a little toning up, shouldn't you start feeding yourself from God's Word every day? Shouldn't you start taking full advantage of study groups and Bible classes? Shouldn't you make the changes necessary to lead you into learning to love God with all your mind, programming it according to His will?

The Acid Test

When scientists need to determine the authenticity of certain materials, they put them in an acid bath. The acid burns away all other materials and leaves only the genuine, if there is any.

It's time for you to take an acid test to find out if the love you offer to God with your mind is genuine. Here's the test:

> When was the last time you decided not to watch or read something, even though you knew you could "get away with it," because you knew it would be programming the wrong material into your mind?

Application

Do you really love God with all your mind? Are you really giving your whole mind as an offering to Him? Are you being careful not to program negative influences into the spiritual computer of your mind? Remember the old computer maxim, "Garbage in, garbage out." As Jesus said, "The good man brings good things out of the good stored up in his heart, and the evil man brings evil things out of the evil stored up in his heart. For out of the overflow of his heart his mouth speaks."[9]

Are you filling your heart and mind with holy and righteous thoughts and influences? Are you using your intellect in creative ways to carry out God's will for your life and to battle Satan and his demonic forces? How are you programming your mind?

Remember, it's war. There is no neutrality. Whose side are you on?

Process and Output

1. Describe the power of the mind by choosing the analogies that most closely define that power:
   _____ electric power outlet
   _____ nuclear energy plant
   _____ IBM computer
   _____ Earnest P. Worrell
   _____ Porsche turbo engine
   _____ other: _____

2. Draw a picture of your spiritual snapshot at the present time as taken by the $1 million dollar camera:

3. Surprise yourself with the power of your mind. In the next five minutes, memorize completely Philippians 4:8.

4. Write a poem or song to God, revealing to Him how you plan to love Him with more of your mind during the next three months.

ENDNOTES

1. 2 Corinthians 10:3-4; 1 Timothy 1:18; 1 Peter 2:11.
2. Matthew 12:30.
3. Joshua 24:15. For further reading on Satan's weapons see The Screwtape Letters by C. S. Lewis.
4. *This Present Darkness* and *Piercing the Darkness* by Frank Peretti. See also *The Prophet* and *The Cooper Kids Adventure Series.*
5. Mark 12:30.
6. Literal translation from Greek text.
7. Ephesians 4:22-24.
8. Ephesians 4:23-24.
9. Luke 6:45.

9 Bodybuilding

The Heisman Trophy. College football's greatest player. The record books rewritten at Auburn University. Yes, Bo Jackson was one of a kind on the collegiate gridiron. And then came the 1986 NFL draft. Everyone knew Bo would go in the first round, and the price tag would be very large. He did, and it was. But surprise, surprise, Bo said no. Bo no's! Instead, Jackson had his eye on a major league baseball career. He signed with the Kansas City Royals and was sent to the class AA club in Memphis, Tenn.

Not long afterward, reports by sportswriters and teammates revealed that Bo was not working very hard. He had natural ability and was incredibly strong, but he seemed to rely on the prestige of his name and his past success in football to keep him in the starting lineup. In September, he was promoted to the majors and began playing with the Royals. Some of the veteran players were disgusted by what seemed to be a prima donna attitude in Bo. He had so much potential and raw ability, but he was too busy basking in his past glory and present status to concentrate fully on improving his performance.

Then something happened. During the winter, Bo decided it was time to quit settling for mediocrity. He wanted to find out what he was really made of. Bo went to the Florida instructional baseball league and played. He worked out with the Auburn University baseball team. He pumped iron. He ran. He put in extra hours with the Royals during spring training. "He's worked very hard," said Manager Billy Gardner. "He's out there every morning at 8:30 taking extra fly balls. Sometimes he will stay after practice and take more fly balls."

Bo even acknowledged that he could have worked harder the previous season than he did. "I could have put more pep in my effort," he said. "I've never really had to work for anything in my life. It was always there. It was simple." But then Bo hit the big leagues. He was no longer the most talented and most experienced guy on the field. He faced a decision — settle for mediocrity or work toward greatness. Bo made his decision. In his own words, "I never set my goals low. I put them at the top of the ladder and go for them." And you know the rest of the story. So does Bo. Bo knows!

The Bo Jackson story reveals an individual who utilized every ounce of energy and strength to accomplish his task. Not only is he playing professional baseball with the Chicago White Sox, but he also became a standout in professional football. He gives it his all. Nothing is held back. He sacrifices his body. He concentrates with his mind. He constantly seeks new ways to perform better. This is exactly the kind of effort Jesus had in mind in Mark 12:30 when He said, "Love the Lord your God with ... all your **strength**." This is the final module of the *JesusPerfect* program for life.

Patient Zero ————————————————

Others in the world have also given every ounce of their energy to something they believe in. And usually when someone gives his or her all to a task, many people are affected. Take Gaetan Dugas as an example. Gaetan appeared to be an ordinary man, but he had a profound impact on the whole world; unfortunately it was negative.

This French Canadian from Quebec City worked as an airline flight steward. While off work, he would go to gay bars or bathhouses and seek out sexual partners. Dugas told one researcher that over a ten-year period, he had made approximately 2,500 homosexual contacts.

Dugas was identified by name in Randy Shilts's monumental study of the AIDS epidemic, *And the Band Played On*. Of the 248 American homosexuals diagnosed as having AIDS in 1982, at least 40 had been sexually involved either with Dugas or with someone else who had. For medical researchers, he was a missing link, "the human explosive whose promiscuous presence may have triggered an epidemic beyond his imagining."[2] Dugas, who died of AIDS in 1984 at the age of 32, is now known as the man who catapulted the AIDS epidemic across America — Patient Zero.

Isn't it sad to realize the negative effect that one man has had on so many thousands of people? All because the man used his strength and energies in the wrong way. It is just as sad to realize that Christians can have an even greater positive impact on society, yet many of us have settled for mediocrity. We seem content to just "get by." We serve mostly when it's comfortable to do so. We don't go about seeking service that takes us away from our comfort zones. We read our Bibles only when we have spare time. We pray, but usually just before meals. We attend church services, but never care for the sick or feed the hungry.[3] Are we really loving God with all our strength? Are we really giving our all to the most important task we face on earth?

> *When you want to love God with all your strength, as much as a drowning man wants air, you will be on your way to becoming a pumped-up, strong and consistent bodybuilding servant for the Lord.*

I am thankful for the teens at the Pleasant Ridge Church of Christ in Arlington, Texas. They have learned that loving God with all their strength entails not only participating in worship assemblies with other Christians or studying their Bibles daily, but also getting out into the streets and touching the lives of poor and needy people. These teens decided to save their snack money for six months. They collected $1,500, with which they bought lawn mowers, weed eaters, rakes and a trailer. They then began a service project titled "Fun in the Son" and took a different crew of teen workers out every Tuesday and Friday during the entire summer to mow lawns for widows and disadvantaged people.

One day each week was spent working for disadvantaged Christians (widows, elderly, sick, etc.). The other day was set aside to serve the community. The kids chose to tackle the seven oversized lots on which the Salvation Army was housing homeless families. Salvation Army Shelter Director David West was impressed and appreciative. "These kids have helped out fantastically," he said. "Our yard will never make *House and Garden*, but it looks nice enough to protect our clients' dignity, and it's neat enough to provide our children with a safe place to play."

The teens also decided to take care of the lawn at Welcome House, a teen crisis center. Cyndee Cashman, coordinator for volunteer services at Welcome House, said, "The teens' efforts have made a difference. Since we offer our services to families at no charge, our limited budget does not allow us the luxury of lawn care. This group of kids has made such a difference in the appearance of Welcome House. We are so grateful that they chose us to receive their services this summer."

The ninety-two teenagers who served on "Fun in the Son" also drew the attention of the media. A front page news article, including color photos, was printed in the *Arlington Citizen-Journal*. Letters came in from community leaders and citizens across the Dallas-Fort Worth Metroplex. Some even sent unsolicited donations to the project. Other churches began developing similar projects for their youth groups. All because a group of teenagers decided to love God with all their strength!

As eighteen-year-old Jonathon Smith said, "I feel we are getting something done at a time when no one else could do it. It's a lot better than playing Nintendo all day and the people are so thankful. One widow insisted on making us cookies." Sixteen-year-old Christina Pyktel summed it up: "We've learned it is a joy serving others!" They're loving God, serving the disadvantaged, and channeling energy in a positive direction.

Bodybuilding

For a tennis player to develop a stronger serve, he must strengthen the muscles in his arm, shoulder and back. For you to develop a stronger serve, you must be willing to do some bodybuilding — spiritual bodybuilding, that is. If you want to love God with all of your strength, here are three suggestions that you might find useful:

First, **define your direction**. If you are planning a trip, you look at a map to determine the best route that will lead you to your destination. It's the same spiritually. Decide where you want to go, how you want to be. Involve yourself in a detailed study of the gospels (Matthew, Mark, Luke and John) concerning the life of Jesus. He is the perfect model. Then develop a workout plan that will build up your weak characteristics and maintain or strengthen your strong traits. This body building program must consist of you as the trainee and God as the trainer. You cannot do it on your own. It takes both of you working as a team. Give your whole life to God, and admit your weaknesses to him. He will help you grow stronger with each passing day. Don't be afraid to update or restructure your workout plan if you find it to be unrealistic or unproductive. Monitor your progress, and keep your finger on your spiritual pulse. And remember, results may not be noticeable overnight. But if you are consistent, the results of your spiritual bodybuilding will become evident to you as well as to everyone else.

Second, **make up your mind that you will reach your destination.** Forget failures from the past. Rise above mediocrity. Your goal is set — go for it! Many years ago, a certain young boy struggled to learn to read. He didn't learn the English alphabet until he was nine years old. Doctors diagnosed him as having dyslexia — seeing words and letters backward. They gave him no hope. But this young man defined the direction he wanted to go and made up his mind to reach that destination. He later became the president of Princeton University, then the governor of New Jersey, and finally president of the United States of America. His name was Woodrow Wilson. And at his death, he was considered to be a master of the English language. He made up his mind and didn't allow obstacles to stop him. You can do the same in developing your spiritual strength. Remember, you have God, the Power Source of the universe, on your side.

Third, **give it all you've got!** Reach down inside and pull out every ounce of energy God has given you. Redirect some of the ways you are using your energy so that more is given to your spiritual body building. Mow a sick neighbor's yard. Take a glass of cold water to the garbage collector. Spend an afternoon at the children's hospital. Write someone a note of thanks. Help your mother with household chores. Pray when there is no food in front of your face. Look for ways to serve. Don't just feel sympathy, do something about it![4] Become obsessed with the desire to serve.

Socrates, the ancient Greek philosopher, was once approached by a young man who asked, "What can I do to become a learned man?"

Socrates immediately took the boy to the town fountain, grabbed him by the neck, and shoved the lad's head under the water. After several seconds of struggle, the young man wrestled free from Socrates grasp and came up gasping for air. Socrates then asked the boy, "While you were under the water, what was the one thing you wanted more than anything else in the world?"

The young man replied, "Air!"

The wise Socrates then said, "Young man, when you want knowledge as much as a drowning man wants air, you will be on your way to becoming a learned man."

When you want to love God with all your strength, as much as a drowning man wants air, you will be on your way to becoming a pumped-up, strong and consistent servant for the Lord.

Application

So far in this book, you've learned that, like a computer, you must be plugged in to the power in order to function as a Christian. That power is found in Jesus Christ. But plugging in is not enough. You then must load God's program for life eternal life. We've called that the *JesusPerfect* program. This program consists of the command of Jesus in Mark 12:30: "Love the Lord your God with all your heart and with all your soul and with all your mind and with all your strength." We have studied each of these characteristics in detail in this second section. But there is one more function of a computer, likewise of a Christian, to which we must now turn our attention. As we move into the third and final section, it's time to print out in to action!

Process and Output

1. If Bo Jackson knows baseball, football, tennis, golf, guitar, sneakers, and even Diddley, but does not know Jesus Christ, has he achieved the greatest accomplishment in life? Why or why not?

2. Is it possible for one single Christian to have as large an impact on society as Gaetan Dugas has had? If you answered yes, describe in detail what that Christian would need to do to have that kind of impact. If no, tell why not.

3. Fill in the following Spiritual Body Building Workout Chart after much prayer and consideration:

Spiritual Bodybuilding Workout Chart

A. Define your direction. My weaknesses are: _____

_____

My strengths are: _____

_____

I want to become: _____

_____

God, please help me. _____

_____

B. Make up your mind that you will reach your destination.
I am going to write each failure from my past on a separate piece of paper and then burn each one up in an "anxiety fire." Here are the past failures I will burn:

These past failures will no longer hold me back. God, please help me.

C. Give it all you've got!
I am going to rechannel my energy deposits. I am going to spend less time doing these things:

I am going to spend more time doing these things:

I pledge to do this with all my strength for the next three months. I will conduct a spiritual fitness evaluation to determine if my body building plan needs restructuring. And God, please help me!

Date _____

Signed_____

ENDNOTES

1. The four main levels of professional baseball are A, AA, AAA, and then the major leagues.
2. "Patient Zero," *People,* Dec. 28, 1987 - Jan. 4, 1988, p.47.
3. Matthew 25:31-46.
4. James 2:14-17.

Section 3
Luke 4:16-21
Print Out
in to Action!

10 Print Out in to Action

During my two years of playing football at Harding University, I must have caught 50,000 passes. Every day, my receiver coach would throw fifty or so passes in my direction. Each night, I would lie on my back in my dorm room and toss and catch a football another one hundred times — each time focusing my eyes on the center of the ball and watching it all the way into my hands. Three years of college baseball added yet another one million balls caught. Needless to say, whenever a bird flew overhead, my hands immediately went up into the air just out of reflex! This reflexive response later generated one of the most humiliating experiences I have ever had.

I played my final collegiate baseball game in May 1984. Married one week later, I moved to Marianna, Ark., to be a full-time minister. Some other Christian men in the area had formed a referee squad for high school football. They invited me to join them and I gladly accepted. I bought some white pants, a black and white striped shirt, a black hat, a yellow flag, and a whistle. Then it came time for the first game of the season.

To say that I was nervous is putting it mildly. The two teams playing that night were 5A schools — the largest in the state. There were approximately two thousand fans present including about a dozen college scouts and coaches. The number-one high school lineman in the country, Freddie Childress, played for the home team. This was not my idea of a good first game to referee. Why couldn't it have been a small school playing on a makeshift cow pasture with only one hundred fans present even when the whole town turned out? Well, my referee buddies were wise. They placed me at the back judge position. This is the referee who stands behind the defensive backs and basically has only two calls to watch for — touchdown and pass interference. There was no way I could mess up a call from that position.

The first quarter went by without a hitch. Then the second. At half-time, I was feeling pretty good about this refereeing business. By the time the third quarter was complete, I had called two touchdowns and was feeling very confident about my ability to referee a football game. "This is easy. I'll do this anytime, anywhere, for $35 a game!" The fourth quarter started and was half over. The score was tied at 6-6. That's when it happened.

> *You can't be a Christian and not be active in doing God's work. You see, Christianity is not a spectator sport!*

The home team had the ball on its own thirty-yard line. The quarter-back took the snap from the center and dropped back for a pass. I noticed the left receiver running a post pattern downfield. He passed the defensive safety and broke open about forty yards downfield. There was no one around him. He had "touchdown" written all over his face. I knew to stay as deep as the deepest man on the field, so I stayed right with the receiver as he began to look back for the ball. (Now let me remind you about the 50,000 footballs and one million baseballs I had caught in college. Remember the bird reflex?)

That's when I noticed that the quarterback had released a perfect spi-raling pass that was coming directly at me fifty yards downfield. If you had been sitting in the stands that night, you would have seen a man standing in the middle of the football field wearing white pants, a striped shirt, a black hat, a yellow flag sticking out of his pocket, with a whistle around his neck, holding his arms straight up in the air and focusing his eyes intensely on the football preparing to make a perfect catch. Can you blame me? It was second nature. Reflex. The crowd gasped. The college scouts dropped their pencils. The ball was about five feet from my fingertips when I realized, "I'm the referee! I'm not supposed to be catching this ball!"

I immediately did a belly-flop on the ground. I didn't touch the ball. But I had made the perfect defensive play by blocking the vision of the receiver directly behind me with my arms. He never saw the ball until the last second.

By then it was too late. The football bounced off his chest with a thud and landed on the ground. The crowd went wild. One thousand spectators were contemplating murder and were being held back by the police, while the other thousand fans were singing my praises. The college scouts and coaches were rolling down the aisles in side-splitting laughter. The coach of the home team was being restrained by my four referee buddies and he was inventing new curse words with every breath. Meanwhile, I continued to lie on my belly with my face buried in the grass. I was praying this prayer: "Lord, if You are ever going to perform a unique miracle in the Twentieth Century, please make me a worm right now!"

Spectator vs. Participant

Why do you think that experience happened to me? Because I'm such a nerd? It would be logical to conclude that. But actually, I believe it happened because of my past involvement. I had played sports since I was six years old. I had always been a participant in the game. I was never a spectator. To this day, I still want to be a participant. When I go to the Texas Rangers games, I want to be out there on the mound pitching instead of watching Nolan Ryan. It is hard for me to watch high school football games because I want so badly to be out there in the game.

Isn't this how it should be with Christianity? Shouldn't you, a Christian, be a participant and not just a spectator? The Bible says that faith without action is dead.[1] You can't be a Christian and not be active in doing God's work. You see, Christianity is not a spectator sport!

Print Out in to Action

Think back to the analogy of a computer. You buy a computer, plug it in to its power source, and then load the program you wish to work on. Suppose you do research for ten years on a treatment for cancer. You load all your findings into your computer and finally find the cure for this dreaded disease. The major medical breakthrough of the century! But you never print out the information. The formula is left in your computer, to which only you have access. You finally die and someone comes along and accidentally erases the formula. What a tragedy! You found the answer to a question that could have saved thousands of lives, but not a single person ever benefitted from your research. Why? You were unwilling to print the answer out for others to see.

It's the same with your spiritual life. You can plug in to the power of Jesus Christ. You can base your life on the *JesusPerfect* program and load all kinds of good spiritual information into the computer of your soul. But what happens if you never print out in to action? What happens if your religion consists of being a good, moral person who doesn't drink, smoke, chew or hang out with those who do; who punches his ticket in the time clock every Sunday morning, Sunday night and Wednesday night, but never reaches out in to the lives of others — especially those who never come to church buildings? The bottom line is clear: If you want to be like Jesus and properly wear the name "Christian," you must be willing to print out in to action not only on Sunday and Wednesday, but also on Monday, Tuesday, Thursday, Friday and Saturday!

The Jesus Model

In Charles Sheldon's classic novel *In His Steps,* one theme dominates the storyline — don't do anything without first asking, "What would Jesus do if He were in my place?" And whatever the answer is, you do it no matter what it costs you or what anybody says. I can think of no greater rule to live by. Jesus is our model for living. He portrays the ultimate example of an active, participating lifestyle. This leads us to our text for the last section of this book. Up to this point, we have been studying from the Gospel of Mark. But for some reason, Mark chose not to write about this experience of Jesus' ministry. Mark takes Jesus from the wilderness straight to Capernaum. But Jesus made a stop before He arrived in Capernaum. Luke provides these details:

> He went to Nazareth, where he had been brought up, and on the Sabbath day he went into the synagogue, as was his custom. And he stood up to read. The scroll of the prophet Isaiah was handed to him. Unrolling it, he found the place where it is written:
> "The Spirit of the Lord is on me, because he has anointed me to preach good news to the poor. He has sent me to proclaim freedom for the prisoners and recovery of sight for the blind, to release the oppressed, to proclaim the year of the Lord's favor." Then he rolled up the scroll, gave it back to the attendant and sat down. The eyes of everyone in the synagogue were fastened on him, and he began by saying to them, "Today this scripture is fulfilled in your hearing."[2]

The Three Principles

Three principles emerge from that text. First, **we must be familiar with the Word of God.** Since Jesus is our model, notice that He knew exactly where to go in the book of Isaiah to find that timely and important passage. There is no doubt that Jesus was very familiar with the Bible of His day — Jewish Scripture. He often quoted from it during His public ministry and even in private, when facing temptation.[3] He evidently had spent many hours from the time He was a youth until He was thirty studying and meditating on Scripture. If Jesus spent that much time in the Word, shouldn't we?

I recently asked a friend what his favorite verse is. He immediately responded by quoting Psalm 119:11, "I have hidden Your word in my heart that I might not sin against you." Could that have been a favorite verse of Jesus? We don't know. But one thing is certain — He believed in this principle!

The second principle that emerges from our text is that **there comes a time for us to shut the Bible and live it.** Again, we see Jesus doing this exact thing. When He finished reading about His mission, Jesus rolled up the scroll and gave it to the synagogue attendant. The next thing we see Him doing is actively participating in the mission He had read about. To spend quantity and quality time in the Word of God is essential, but to learn it without living it is tragic. I can pay an atheist to memorize the Bible, but that doesn't mean he will live it and positively affect the lives of other people. Are you wearing your Bible out through Christian living?

The third and final principle found within our text is that **true Christlike living requires active participation in the lives of disadvantaged people.** Take a look at the five traits Jesus defined His mission by and circle the word in the brackets that best describes each one:

1. Preach good news to the poor. [active or passive]
2. Proclaim freedom for the prisoners. [active or passive]
3. Proclaim recovery of sight for the blind. [active or passive]
4. Release the oppressed. [active or passive]
5. Proclaim the year of the Lord's favor. [active or passive]

If I were to ask you to sum up the mission of Jesus with one word, what word would you use? If you chose the word "active", you definitely have understood the message of Luke 4:16-21. Jesus, as your model, portrays to you the principles that should guide your life for as long as you live on this earth.

Application

Being a spectator is not enough in Christianity. Passive Christianity is an oxymoron (like "jumbo shrimp," "cold heat" or "painless dentist"). It just doesn't fit the definition. Christianity requires getting involved in the game. Specifically, it means spending time reading your mission as recorded in the Word, getting out and living the mission taught to you through the Word, and involving yourself actively in the lives of disadvantaged people. Luke 4:16-21 refers to the beginning of the public ministry of Jesus. It's one of the key texts that defines Jesus' mission on earth. Since our goal is to be like Jesus, we are therefore called by God through this text to:

> 1. Teach the good news to the poor, informing them of the spiritual riches available in Christ. It's not enough to just clothe, shelter and feed them.
> 2. Proclaim freedom for the prisoners of sin by pointing them toward the glorious resurrection — the free gift of love (the ultimate electric outlet).
> 3. Offer sight to the blind by sharing with them your light, your source of power, Jesus Christ (overcoming darkness).
> 4. Comfort the oppressed by pointing them to the Great Physician, the healer of sin-sickness and sorrow.
> 5. Proclaim Jesus to all the world, for that is your great commission.[4]

Remember, a church pew is similar to a bleacher or a box seat in a stadium. If it's the only place you "practice your Christianity," you are *not* a contributing part of God's team. His team consists of active participants who are involved in life. Why not join the winners and *print out in to action*!

Process and Output

1. One of the principles discussed in this chapter is the need to be familiar with the Word of God. List five scriptures that are key texts for you in living the Christian life:

   a.)

   b.)

   c.)

   d.)

   e.)

2. John the Baptist was in prison when he heard that Jesus had begun His ministry. John sent messengers to find out the details:

   > "Go back and report to John what you hear and see: The blind receive sight, the lame walk, those who have leprosy are cured, the deaf hear, the dead are raised, and the good news is preached to the poor." (Matthew 11:4-5)

   Compare Jesus' response to John's messengers with what you have learned from Luke 4:16-21. What are the similarities, and what does this lead you to conclude about Jesus' mission?

3. Read Matthew 25:31-46. In that passage, Jesus describes activities of His true followers. How do those activities compare to those in the two texts mentioned in number two above?

What does this tell you personally about your priorities as a Christian?

4. List five things you plan to do consistently over the next three months to print out in to action for Jesus Christ:

1.)
2.)
3.)
4.)
5.)

ENDNOTES

1. James 2:14-17; Matthew 25:31-46.
2. Luke 4:16-21.
3. See Matthew 4:1-11; Luke 4:1-12.
4. See Matthew 28:18-20; Mark 16:15-16.

11 The Mexico Mission: A Case Study

"A gentle mist is floating effortlessly through the Mexican night. I am in one of the seven vans escorting our team of teenagers and adult sponsors from the airport to the Hotel Aranzazu in inner-city Guadalajara.

"As I look out the foggy window, I see an old city radiating a luring fragrance of history and Spanish romance. Cobblestone streets. Horse-drawn carriages. Three-hundred-year-old cathedrals trimmed with gold. A mysterious city that seems to whisper, 'You are my guest. Admire me, enjoy my beauty, and drink from the cup of my ancient stories and lore.'

"Our group, consisting of seventeen teenagers and six adults from the Pleasant Ridge church in Arlington and thirty teens and six adults from the Highland church in Abilene, is somewhat tired, but the excitement of our arrival has sparked each individual. Tomorrow promises to be an eventful day. I will save my ink for then."

The above was my journal entry from a recent mission trip. It referenced the first day of a week-long campaign held in the inner-city area of Guadalajara, Mexico. The unique thing about this campaign was that it was carried out mostly by teenagers.

During the week, I saw several of those teens do some fantastic things. One day at lunch, I noticed two girls slipping dinner rolls into their pockets while they thought no one was looking. Later in the evening, they quietly excused themselves and went out into the back allies looking for street beggars to whom they gave the bread "in the name of Jesus Christ."

There was also the teenage boy who brought back to the hotel a young street orphan whose body was mangled, deformed and malnourished. The teenage boy took care of the orphan's needs and offered the little boy friendship.

Then there was the group of teenagers who left three packed suitcases full of their clothing to be given to the poor people of the city. Those beggars, the little street orphan, and the poor people who received the clothes saw Jesus, many for the first time, through the actions of those teenagers. Those teens, as well as the adult sponsors, opened their lives to the will of God and many Mexicans were positively influenced as a result. They printed out in to action!

The "Impaired" Mentality

As you read about this concept of printing out in to action for the Lord, you may be thinking, "I can't do that. I'm not talented enough. I don't have the resources. I'm not ready yet. I just need to study more or wait until I'm older. Then I can really do a lot for the Lord." I call that an impaired mentality. Some teenagers live as if they are physically, mentally and spiritually incapable of serving.

Anselmo was that way. He was a man living without God. He had no hope. No peace. He also struggled with an impairment that confined him to a wheelchair. He felt robbed of the quality of life that most people take for granted. But Anselmo's life changed.

During a Herald of Truth Harvest Campaign in Mexico, much like the one our mission team was involved with, Anselmo was converted to Christ. Almost immediately, he decided to dedicate the rest of his life to preaching the Good News of Jesus Christ.

Anselmo enrolled in the Monterey School of Preaching and spent the next three years preparing for his ministry. While there, he met a young woman named Juana. The two were married and now have several handsome children. They named their first child after Jesus — Jesus Anselmo.

Today Anselmo is serving full time as a minister. He hooks up his wheelchair to a motorcycle and hits the streets every day looking for people with whom to share the Gospel. One of his favorite passages in the Bible is Philippians 4:13: "I can do everything through [Christ] who gives me strength." Even though Anselmo will never walk or run, he no longer considers himself impaired. Rather, he considers himself blessed to be able to serve the Lord. Anselmo is a good example of a person who is printing out in to action.

The Golden Opportunity

It's time that teenagers all over the world join together in actively proclaiming Jesus Christ to the world. To do your part, you must realize there is no waiting list for service in God's kingdom. He allows no such list. You must also realize that a golden opportunity is available to you now as a teenager.

> *If all the teenagers in the world who called themselves Christians would seize the golden opportunity within their grasp, unbelievable numbers of people would be saved from the treacherous clutches of sin.*

You see, teenagers have lots of energy that can be put to use serving God. Teens have the special opportunity to live out a full lifetime of service for the Lord. Teens are still flexible and moldable, unlike many adults who are set in their ways. Teens have the greatest possibility of leading their peer group to God. All these factors define a golden opportunity that rests within your hands. You can make the most of it and print out in to action, or you can let it slip through your fingers like sand to be blown away by the winds of time.

If all the teenagers in the world who called themselves Christians would seize the golden opportunity within their grasp, unbelievable numbers of people would be saved from the treacherous clutches of sin. To give you an idea of the numbers I am referring to, consider some recent statistics from the Domino's Pizza chain:

1. During one year, Domino's produced 200,000,000 pizzas. That comes out to 6.3 pizzas per second, every second of the day. That is 3.8 million pizzas per week!

2. During one year, Domino's Pizza drivers traveled an estimated 1,643,836 miles each day — approximately half the Pioneer 10 spacecraft's eleven-year voyage.

3. In one year, Domino's Pizza drivers accumulated more than 600,000,000 miles, which is three times the length of the tail of the Great Comet of 1843.

4. If all the Domino's pizza boxes used in one year were stacked in a pile, they would be 22,900,000 feet tall, which is more than 18,000 times the height of the Empire State Building, 800 times the height of Mount Everest, and more than 1,000 times the height of Mount McKinley.

5. In one year, Domino's used 22,243,000 pounds of pepperoni. If each slice were laid side by side, they would make a chain over 136,000 miles long, which is more than half the distance above the earth of the Apollo 8 mission!

Incredible statistics, aren't they? I have news for you. Domino's Pizza is not half as big as God's church can be! The influence of Domino's Pizza cannot even begin to compare to the potential influence of the children of God.

Remember what happened on the day of Pentecost in Acts 2? Three thousand people became Christians in one day.[1] They were so excited about sharing the Good News, that more people became Christians every day.[2]

The success of Domino's Pizza will pale in comparison to the success God will work through the church when you and I and everyone else who calls himself Christian decides to start printing out in to action for Jesus Christ! But it is a sad fact that many teenagers who call themselves Christians get more excited about pizza than they do about serving God.

Application

I began this chapter with a personal journal entry from the first day of a Mexico Mission Campaign. In closing I would like to show you my journal entry from the second day of that trip:

"For three hours this morning, we distributed brochures to every hand that would receive one. A cold tropical rain flooded the streets of Guadalajara, but the rain didn't dampen the spirits of the determined teens and sponsors who were so eager to invite people to hear the Good News of Jesus Christ. As I reflect back to those first three hours on the streets, four observations come to mind:

"1. **Anybody can carry out the Great Commission of Jesus**, even those who cannot preach, teach or memorize Scripture. Anybody can stand on a street corner, smile and hand out pieces of paper! It is so simple. And the irony is that it does so much for me. It makes me feel so good about myself. It helps my faith to grow. It's one way for me to confess Christ and the confession that Jesus is Lord (verbally and non-verbally) is the core of the Gospel. It is a confession that needs to be made daily within my life and it will point people toward the Savior.

"2. **I see the beauty of God's creation and the way He can implement His kingdom into various cultures using different methods.** God is continually creating and consistently adapting. That means that *God is in control no matter where I go.* Sure, it's scary to go to a country where I'm the foreigner. I am in the minority here. Sure, anything could happen. But when I realize that God is in control, there is no place on earth that I could go and not have God at my side and in my heart. Thank you, Almighty Father!

"3. **There is no way of knowing how much good could come from the handing out of one soggy, little brochure to a peasant on the street corner in Mexico.** The recipient reads it, attends the meeting, hears the Gospel, becomes a Christian, converts others who in turn convert others, and a congregation of the Lord's church is established. It has happened before and it will happen again — it could be right here in Guadalajara! One thing is certain — brochures handed out might be seeds planted through which God will give the increase.

"4. Finally, **I realize how much I want my little daughter to serve God**. This morning I saw several precious, little, dark-haired Mexican girls with big, beautiful, brown eyes. They would look up at me with snaggle-tooth grins and a sweet innocence glowed from them. Those little girls will grow up and make choices about the God they allow into their lives. They will marry and raise children of their own and greatly influence the eternal destiny of many. So will you, my little Christin Michelle Sites. Please tell little girls about Jesus. And please tell mommies and daddies everywhere about the Lord who loves them. Show them the joy and peace that comes from knowing Christ and the power of the resurrection. I pray with all my heart that you will dedicate your life to sharing the Good News with as many as possible all over the world, just as the teens and sponsors have done on this trip. It's the least you can do for Jesus and it's exhilarating!"

Many are joining together in such efforts as the Mexico Mission Campaign to go into Third World countries and spread the Good News of Jesus Christ. The groups of teenagers I personally lead have doubled in size every year. I know hundreds, even thousands, of teenagers who view their lives on this earth as missions for God. But it's going to take all of us joining together in one body[3] to have the ultimate impact on the world that we can possibly have. And you don't have to go to another country to do it. The mission field begins in your own school and neighborhood. The church needs you. Are you willing? Will you join us as we print out in to action for the Lord?

Process and Output

1. What kind of insights do you think you would gain if you traveled to a Third World country, and how would your perspective on life change?

2. Why do some people feel impaired when it comes to actively serving for Jesus Christ?

   List some things that you personally can do to help someone overcome his or her feeling of spiritual impairment:

3. How did you feel when you read the Domino's Pizza statistics and then thought about the impact the church is having?

4. I'm sure you realize you don't have to travel to a Third World country to be a missionary. You also don't have to live in a grass hut and eat grub worms. You can find people in your own hometown who desperately need to be touched by the compassionate hand of Jesus. After prayer and consideration, write down how you plan to carry out your mission of love to those people over the next three months:

STEP 1:

STEP 2:

STEP 3:

STEP 4:

ENDNOTES

1. Acts 2:41.
2. Acts 2:47.
3. See Ephesians 4:4.

12 Flashback

"Click, click, click." I put both hands over my eyes and gritted my teeth like a pair of vise grips tightened down all the way. *"Click, click, click."* I peeked through an opening between two of my fingers and concluded we were about 150 feet high. I could see the teens in my youth group standing below, waving at me and laughing at my display of bravery. The roller coaster cars were slowly being pulled up the track to the starting point — backward! The track was so steep that it seemed as if we were looking straight down at the earth below us.

"Click, click, click." I knew that at any moment there was going to be a pause. The clicks would stop, the cars would be motionless for a split second, and then every set of tonsils on the roller coaster track would be in complete view. My hunch was correct. *"Pause. Deathly silence."* Then down we went for the 150-foot drop at warp speed, screaming as if we had seen a castle full of vampires. I'm not sure, but I think my heart and eyeballs actually reached the bottom before the car I was sitting in did. At least that's what the teens in the youth group said!

We soared through the double loop-to-loop in no time flat, and before I could even convince myself to stop yelling, we were already slowly ascending another steep hill — this time with our backs to the ground and our faces to the heavens. *"Click, click, click."* That sure sounded familiar. *"Click, click, click."* I began to hyperventilate. *"Click, click, click."* I cupped my hands over my mouth and muttered to Mandy that I had enjoyed our six years of marriage together. Then came the nauseating pause — the one where the clicks stop and time stands still for a moment. Then the tonsil demonstration did an encore. Down we went — this time backward! We must have broken the sound barrier about the time we reached the double loop-to-loop.

Between screams I was thinking, "Didn't this just happen?" It was like watching an instant replay at a football game — except backward. Maybe that's why the folks at Six Flags Over Texas decided to call this roller coaster "Flashback."

When we finally came to a stop, one of the workers helped pry my right hand loose from the bar at the front of the car and my left hand from Mandy's knee. When I could finally speak a couple of minutes later, I vowed never again to set foot on that roller coaster.

Well, I've ridden Flashback several more times since that first experience. And I must admit that I still hyperventilate about half the time. I always make the same vow each time I get off. But if history repeats itself, I will go back again and again. So don't be surprised if you ever go to Six Flags and hear someone scream, "It's been great knowing you, Mandy!"

Flashback

I'm not going to try persuading you to ride a roller coaster with me (you would probably be too embarrassed anyway), but I do want us to experience a flashback of another sort. In doing so, we'll get another perspective on what it means to print out in to action for the Lord.

Let's go back to two concepts that have already been discussed in Chapters 3 through 5 — the messages of the cross and the resurrection of Jesus Christ. Two statements stand out:

> *Contrary to the polished, gold-plated emphasis most people place on Golgotha today, the cross of Christ actually portrays the ugliness of sin.*

> *For too long, many Christians have been focusing their gaze only on the cross. It's time we leap with joy in front of the empty tomb!*

One day a minister friend of mine sat in my office and said,

"Everything we do as Christians centers on the cross. Every sermon I preach must contain the message of the cross." He then quoted 1 Corinthians 2:2: "For I resolved to know nothing while I was with you except Jesus Christ and him crucified."

I agree wholeheartedly with my friend, but only if his perspective of the cross includes the resurrection. The same apostle Paul who wrote the verse mentioned above also wrote, just a few chapters later: "And if Christ has not been raised, our preaching is useless and so is your faith."[1] In another letter, Paul also wrote: "I want to know Christ and the power of his resurrection."[2]

The cross without the resurrection spells defeat. The resurrection without the cross spells inattention to sin. They go hand in hand. If every sermon preached must contain the message of the cross, it must also contain the message of the resurrection! It's not fair to look at only one side of the coin. Every coin has two sides that are inseparable. It cannot be a complete coin without containing both sides. And it's the same with the cross and the resurrection of Jesus Christ.

Balance

I have noticed that the symbol of the cross can be found almost everywhere: cross-shaped earrings and necklaces, steeples with a cross on top, baptistries in the shape of a cross, gold crosses engraved on Bible covers, small crosses to be carried in pockets, church auditoriums set up in the shape of a cross, pulpits shaped like a cross, crosses hanging from car mirrors, even baseball players making the sign of the cross before batting. There are crosses everywhere!

But where are the symbols of the empty tomb? If a symbol of the cross is so helpful in reminding us about the death of Christ, wouldn't a symbol of the empty tomb help to remind us of the life of Christ? Imagine how having a balanced view of the cross and resurrection of Jesus Christ would affect our worship. There would be time for somber, quiet reflection regarding the incredible sacrifice Jesus made for us. There would also be a time of joyful celebration because of the fact He rose from the grave and freed us from our captivity to sin!

A good example of this balance, or the lack of it, is found in the way you observe the Lord's Supper. If you focus mainly on the cross, you probably work hard at picturing Jesus on the cross as you partake of Communion. You probably do it individually and very quietly, for that's proper at a memorial service.

If you include in your thinking the fact that Jesus Christ rose from the dead, however, you will not only think back to Jesus hanging on a cross, but you will also see Him bursting forth from the empty tomb. You will be joyful that death could not hold Jesus. You will be proclaiming, by partaking of the Lord's Supper, that Jesus is currently alive and present within the church, within the people who are sitting right next to you on the church pew.

In partaking of the Lord's Supper with this balanced perspective, you affirm, along with the congregation of believers, that you believe Jesus died **and** rose. The Lord's Supper then becomes as much a shared event as it is an individual event. You think not only of the past, but also the present. And then you remember the verse that came from the lips of Jesus Himself: "I tell you, I will not drink of this fruit of the vine from now on until that day when I drink it anew with you in my Father's kingdom."[3] In partaking of the Lord's Supper, you are also proclaiming a future event — the return of the Lord for His people.

> *If we can learn to walk the walk and talk the talk of the cross and the resurrection during our daily living and worship, we will make a positive difference for others.*

Participation in the Lord's Supper is only a funeral if the cross is the only focus. But it moves beyond that to include joyful celebration and mutual affirmation when the resurrection is included in the picture. It then points not only to the past, but also to the present and the future.

After all, the original Greek word for the Lord's Supper is *eucharist*, which refers to more than just a quiet time of reflection. It literally means a time of thanksgiving, gratitude and celebration.

The Big Picture

Think about this concept of balance in terms of a true story that happened when I was five years old. I remember hearing the story on the five o'clock news by Walter Cronkite, and it scared the daylights out of me.

A boy my same age had been kidnapped from a wealthy family. The captors chloroformed the little boy and buried him alive in a coffin with a twenty-four hour supply of oxygen. Then they sent a ransom note to the parents, demanding a large sum of money.

Imagine if you had been that little boy. You awake to discover you're in total darkness. Damp. Clammy. Musty. You attempt to sit up, and immediately you bump your head. Your hands begin to search, and they discover the lining of the coffin and the oxygen bottle beside you. A horrifying thought flashes in to your mind. This can't be happening! This has to be a nightmare! You realize you are six feet under, and death is your certain companion.

I am glad to report that the story had a happy ending. The father of the boy paid the ransom, and the kidnappers revealed where the boy was buried. Rescue workers dug through the dirt and found the coffin, lifting the lid and pulling the little fellow up to safety just as his oxygen supply was running out. What an event!

Needless to say, there was great celebration at that moment by all involved. Even now, a quarter of a century later, there is a man somewhere on this earth who is still very thankful that his father was willing to pay the ransom to save his life.

Some important parallels can be drawn between this story and another true story — yours.

You are kidnapped by the Devil and his evil forces. They bury you in a coffin called sin. Dark. Clammy. Musty. Your oxygen supply is dwindling fast. You hold in you hand a one-way ticket to eternity in hell, and there's nothing you can do about it. Panic grabs your neck and squeezes with all its might. The only hope you have rests in the hands of your Father. Will He come through for you? The Father gives the signal, and His Son is nailed to a rugged cross.

The ransom is paid. The stone rolls away. The coffin lid is lifted. And then a hand extends into the penetrating light. You blink the blur out of your eyes, and then you recognize the hand that's reaching in to rescue you. It's a hand with a nail hole in it. You take the hand and are pulled out of your grave of eternal death. Freedom and life fill your lungs. Needless to say, celebration comes naturally for you! Your Father has come through for you.

It's important for you to consider the progression of emotions and reactions involved in each of these stories. Therefore, look at the parallels portrayed in the following chart, and keep in mind that this is the big picture of a balanced view of cross and resurrection:

Kidnapped Boy	Cross & Resurrection
Boy in Coffin — *Somber*	You in Sin's Grave — *Somber*
$ Ransom Paid — *(Boy still in grave) Somber yet with Hope*	✝ Ransom Paid — *(You are still in sin's grave) Somber yet with Hope*
Coffin Opened/Rescue — *Celebration!*	Resurrection/Rescue — *Celebration!*

The ransom would have been meaningless had the coffin/tomb not been opened. May we never be guilty of focusing on only one side of the coin! I pray that you and I will learn to live, both individually and in corporate worship, with a balanced theology of cross and resurrection.

Application

It may seem that this chapter has little to do with printing out in to action. You may think that how you view and participate in the Lord's Supper is only a mental exercise. But that is not the case. How you approach the sacrifice on the cross and the power of the resurrection will have a big impact on how you act and live.

If you approach the cross and resurrection with a balanced view, you will be so full of thanksgiving for what God has done for you that you won't be able to keep it inside. Non-Christians will want to know what it is that makes you different. They will be intrigued by the way you naturally handle the valleys and mountaintops of life. They will sense your balance of quietness, reflection, joy, celebration, and looking to the future for things yet to occur. They will want what you have. If you can learn to walk the walk and talk the talk of the cross and the resurrection during your daily living and worship, you will make a positive difference for others. You will be an example to the world of what it means to live with the big picture always in mind — the picture of the incredible rescue by your Lord and Savior Jesus Christ. Now that's a printout worth reading!

Process and Output

1. At what time in you life did you feel the most trapped in the darkness of sin?

2. List times when celebration has come most naturally for you (or that you predict will come in the future; example: birth of a child; He/She said yes).

Now compare the value of those experiences with the value of God's gift of freedom offered to you through the cross and resurrection. How does it make you feel? (You might write a poem, song, etc., in response.)

3. Design a congregational worship experience that balances cross and resurrection. List song titles, Bible reading texts, sermon topic, and other ideas.

ENDNOTES

1. 1 Corinthians 15:14.
2. Philippians 3:10. It's important to realize that the crucifixion of Jesus took care of sin, but it did not take care of the adversary. The adversary was defeated at the resurrection. Joy was completed when the stone was rolled away.
3. Matthew 26:29.

13 Programming Your Future

He was a normal kid. He enjoyed spending time with his friends. He went to school and took the same classes that all other fourteen-year-olds take. But one thing separated Ray Bateman Jr. from his peers — his presenting a paper on cancer research to the American Federation of Clinical Research in New York City on Oct. 7, 1988. He is the youngest person ever to present a paper to this renowned group of doctors and medical researchers.

It all started when Ray got his first computer at the age of nine. By the time he was eleven, he had attended a computer camp for high school students at Stanford University. At the age of fourteen, Ray was working on his fifth computer — a $23,000 Macintosh complete with laser printer in his own bedroom.

One day, he went to his neighbor's house to visit with his fourteen-year-old friend Terry Tisman. Terry's father, Glenn Tisman, was a doctor who specialized in chemotherapy treatment for patients with colon cancer. Ray became interested in Dr. Tisman's research and found himself talking more with Dr. Tisman than with Terry each time he visited.

Dr. Tisman soon recognized Ray's interest in medicine, as well as his ability with computers. So he invited the fourteen-year-old to do some research for him.

"Working with him was like working with a (post-doctoral) fellow," Dr. Tisman said. "But he's still a kid, basically. My lab technician used to complain that Ray would leave his candy wrappers lying around."

Ray spent more than 1,300 hours researching the project. It has already won seven awards, including first place in the California Science Fair.

"His being so young will surprise some people," Dr. Tisman said.

"But I have confidence in him."

Ray Bateman Jr. is using his skills at a young age to produce positive and helpful results. He plugged his computer in, programmed it, and is definitely printing out in to action! He's a teenager who is making a difference!

The same can happen to you spiritually when you: (1) plug in to the power of God; (2) load the *JesusPerfect* program for life (loving God with all your heart, mind, soul and strength); and (3) print out in to action. It will make a difference in your life and that difference will affect others as well. A transformation will take place.

Transformed

Lew Wallace hated Christianity. He was a famous general and was said to be a literary genius. Because of his deep unbelief in Christianity he and his agnostic friend Robert Ingersoll decided they would write the book that would once-and-for-all destroy the "myth" of Christianity and the story of the Bible. Wallace traveled all over the world, researching in the best libraries known to man. After many months of research, he began to write the book.

> *One cannot truly be in the presence of Jesus without witnessing His transforming power.*

By the time Lew Wallace was writing the second chapter of his book, he found himself on his knees, crying out, "My Lord and my God!" The one whom he had tried to expose as a fraud — Jesus Christ — had captured his heart. Wallace then changed approaches concerning his research and writing and he went on to produce what many consider to be the greatest novel of all time concerning the life and times of Jesus and early

Christianity. Maybe you've seen the movie or read the book *Ben Hur*. Lew Wallace met Jesus for the first time and as a result was transformed from a Bible scoffer to a believing child of God.[1]

Rags to Riches

England's Queen Victoria once visited a paper mill. The foreman at the mill took great pride in showing his guest and her attendant around the factory without even knowing who she was. One of the stops on the tour was at the rag sorting area, where employees picked out the rags from the garbage of the city. Queen Victoria was curious about what would be done with the filthy rags, and she was told that they would make the finest white paper available.

After her departure from the paper mill, the foreman found out who his distinguished guest was. Some time later, the queen received a package of very delicate white stationary with her profile on it. Along with the stationary was a note from the foreman explaining that the precious paper had been made from the dirty rags she had inspected. From rags to riches!

Positive Proof from the Text

The Roman centurion of Mark 15:39, like Lew Wallace, once scoffed at Jesus. He gave the orders to drive the nails. He allowed the kangaroo court and possibly even presided over it. He was in charge of the whole crucifixion. He, like the rags Queen Victoria looked at, was a dirty rag in that trash heap of a hill outside Jerusalem. But despite his gnarled past and the present calloused condition of his heart, that centurion couldn't help but notice something different in this one they called the King of the Jews. *One cannot truly be in the presence of Jesus without witnessing His transforming power.* And notice what the centurion ended up proclaiming at the death of Jesus: "Surely this man was the Son of God!"

An old tradition that has been handed down from at least the third century is that this centurion's name was Longjinus. And as a result of the things he witnessed and the encounter he had with Jesus on the day of the crucifixion, he became a Christian.

It's said that Longjinus later even suffered martyrdom because of his faith in Jesus Christ. He had witnessed the power of Jesus Christ. He plugged in to that power. He programmed his life to love God with all his heart, soul, mind and strength. And if tradition is right, Longjinus printed out in to action in the ultimate way — he gave his life for the One who had died for him.

Transformed from rags to riches by the power of God!

Application

What meaning does all this have for you? Let me sum it up in the following way. It has been estimated that the chemical contents (inorganic compounds) of a 150-pound man were worth $.98 in the 1930s. Because of inflation, that value estimate has been raised to $8.75 in the 1990s (with 60 percent of the body's content being water, which is free). That's less than the price of a cheap pair of sneakers. Really helps your self image, doesn't it!

But there's a different perspective to be considered. People have learned how to harness and utilize the power found within atoms. With this atomic power in view, someone decided to calculate the number of atoms in a human body. The result is that 11,400,000 kilowatts of power per pound could be produced. Using this method of computation, a man weighing 150 pounds is worth $85.5 billion! Feel better?

When you plug in to the power of God, program your future based on the *JesusPerfect* program, and print out in to action, you will be transformed from a person who is spiritually dead to a priceless, blood-bought child of God Himself.

You will become an heir to His kingdom. Your name will be etched on a key to a heavenly mansion. You will not be promised earthly possessions, but you will be given power — the power of God within you. You may never receive an easy road in life, but you will receive the spiritual stamina you need to triumphantly face the trials of life and live in peace and contentment. All the trials of this life will be totally erased by the joy of one day being in the presence of the very power that has sustained you — Jehovah God.

You will no longer have to stay in the coffin of darkness and sin. You will be rescued by the hand you recognize so well — the one with a nail hole in it. You can live each day knowing your future is secure, that God is sculpting your heart, soul and mind, and empowering you with His strength. You can even live with confidence that your life is God's life — that you will even die for Him, as He has already done for you, if the situation arises.

So what are you waiting for? You are already sitting at the computer terminal of your life. You need to plug in to the power of Jesus. Will you? Will you then load the *JesusPerfect* program for life in your soul? Will you love God with all your heart, soul, mind and strength? You need to do this in order to print out in to action for the Lord so that others may be helped by your life. You need to do this for your own sake as well. It's a decision of destiny — **eternal** destiny.

What's your answer? Who will be programming your future?

Process and Output

1. List examples of transformations you have personally witnessed (example: a caterpillar becoming a butterfly):

a.)

b.)

c.)

d.)

2. Read Mark 15:15-39 and Matthew 27:50-54. What caused the Roman centurion to change from a calloused non-believer to a believer in Jesus Christ?

3. Looking back at your answer to number 2, what does it tell you about the power of God? Draw a picture symbolizing this power.

4. If you haven't yet plugged in to the power of God and programmed your life with the *JesusPerfect* program, list the date and time that you plan to do so on the line below:

Date: _____   Time: _____

Now show this to a parent, friend or minister, or call and inform them of your decision to follow Jesus. They'll be happy to help you carry out that decision.

I would also like to know of your decision. Please share it with me by writing to: Christian Communications, P.O. Box 150, Nashville, TN 37202.

ENDNOTES

1. To review this concept go back and read question #2 in the Process and Output section of Chapter 1.

YOU CAN CHANGE THE WORLD

We live in a world today where two out of every three people live in desperate poverty. Children are the hardest hit. Millions of kids receive little or no education, health care or adult guidance. They struggle to survive from day to day. Many give up hope and all sense of self worth at an early age. I have personally visited many of these children in several Third World countries (remember the Mexico Mission trip in chapter 11). I was so moved by the needs of these children that I decided to try to make a difference for at least one.

Jimmy Sites Family

Milene Rosa de Silva

My family and I have supported Milene Rosa de Silva for several years now. She is a needy little girl from South America whom we help through a wonderful child development organization. A highlight for us is to receive pictures and letters from Milene, which we keep in a family scrapbook. Although only six years old, she always communicates her gratefulness to us and lets us know she is praying for us daily. She definitely has become a part of our family. My little girl, Christin, does not say a prayer without mentioning Milene.

You can experience this kind of one-on-one relationship with a child who is in desperate need of your help. You can go to bed at night knowing that you are making a difference for at least one child in the world. You might consider making this an ongoing service project for your youth group or family. Will you join us in reaching out to show a child God's love, and to help make his or her world a better place?

If you are interested in finding out more about how to help a child, please write:

Christian Communications
Attn: Jimmy Sites Child Development Information
P. O. Box 150
Nashville, TN 37710

I HOPE YOU WILL JOIN THE TEAM THAT WILL DARE TO MAKE A DIFFERENCE.

Thanks for taking the
time to read this book.

Jimmy Sites

Additional books by Jimmy Sites:

Plug Into Power
Plug Into Relationships
Satan Stole the Show

Additional books for teens published by Christian Communications:

Don't Kiss Toads, by Sandra Humphrey
Going Through the Motions, by Linda Schott and Marty Dodson
Now What Do I Do?, by Patty Schafer
Straight Talk for Teens, by Randy Simmons
Teens In Two Worlds, by Mike Cope
The Christian College Advantage, by James Woodrow